On
in the GTA

An eclectic guide to the exurban sprawl of Greater Toronto

Drawings and photographs by
Michael J. Seward

Text by
Randall White

eastendbooks
Toronto 2003

Copyright © Michael J. Seward and Randall White, 2003

All rights reserved. No part of this publication may be reproduced, stored in a retrieval system, or transmitted in any form or by any means, electronic, mechanical, photocopying, recording or otherwise (except brief passages for purposes of review), without the prior permission of eastendbooks. Permission to photocopy should be requested from the Canadian Reprography Collective.

Care has been taken to trace the ownership of copyright material used in the text. The authors and publisher welcome any information enabling them to rectify any reference or credit in subsequent editions.

Printed in Canada by Métrolitho

Cover design by Tibor Choleva and Melissa McClellan, Deep Blue Design Co.
Cover drawings by Michael J. Seward.

National Library of Canada Cataloguing in Publication

Seward, Michael J., 1945-
    On the Road in the GTA : an eclectic guide to the exurban sprawl of Greater Toronto / drawings and photographs by Michael J. Seward; text by Randall White.

Includes bibliographical references and index.
ISBN 1-896973-32-9

    1. Toronto Region (Ont.)—Description and travel. 2. Toronto Region (Ont.)—History. 3. Toronto Region (Ont.)—Pictorial works. I. White, Randall II. Title.

FC3097.3.S43 2003   971.3'541   C2003-902744-9

eastendbooks is an imprint of Venture Press
45 Fernwood Park Avenue
Toronto, Ontario, Canada M4E 3E9
(416) 691-6816 [telephone]
(416) 691-2414 [fax]
VISIT OUR WEBSITE AT www.eastendbooks.com

Contents

	What Is It?	5
I	HALTON REGION	9
1	Burlington	11
2	Milton	15
3	Halton Hills	19
4	Oakville	23
II	PEEL REGION	27
5	Mississauga	29
6	Brampton	35
7	Caledon	39
III	YORK REGION	43
8	King	45
9	East Gwillimbury	49
10	Georgina	53
11	Whitchurch-Stouffville	57
12	Newmarket	61
13	Aurora	65
14	Richmond Hill	69
15	Vaughan	73
16	Markham	77
IV	DURHAM REGION	81
17	Pickering	83
18	Ajax	87
19	Uxbridge	91
20	Brock	95
21	Scugog	99
22	Whitby	103
23	Oshawa	107
24	Clarington	111
V	THE CITY OF TORONTO	117
	Note on Sources and Modes of Travel	139
	Index	141

The GTA Today

Area Municipality Populations 2001

City of Toronto	2,481,494	Newmarket	65,788
Mississauga	612,925	Caledon	50,595
Brampton	325,428	Halton Hills	48,184
Markham	208,615	Aurora	40,167
Vaughan	182,022	Georgina	39,263
Burlington	150,836	Milton	31,471
Oakville	144,738	Whitchurch-Stouffville	22,008
Oshawa	139,051	East Gwillimbury	20,555
Richmond Hill	132,030	Scugog	20,173
Whitby	87,413	King	18,533
Pickering	87,139	Uxbridge	17,377
Ajax	73,753	Brock	12,110
Clarington	69,834	**GTA**	**5,081,502**

SOURCE: Statistics Canada.

What Is It?

The present-day Greater Toronto Area or GTA was invented by professionals working for governments and the real estate industry. Then the rest of us followed.

Or at least some of us did. One of the focus-group subjects in our research said, "What does the 'A' in GTA stand for again?"

The subject in question lives in a condo on Bay Street, downtown. But there are similar forms of benign local oblivion much further afield. People who live in such places as Oakville can still be reluctant followers of the professional terminology, so long as they stay at home.

When they travel, however, Toronto or Greater Toronto is where even Oakville residents say they come from nowadays. And of course Toronto is where anyone who lives on Bay Street downtown comes from, without debate at all — even if the person originally came from Saskatchewan, or Nairobi, Hong Kong, Sicily, Hungary, the Punjab, Michigan, or Minnesota, many years ago.

Most of those professionally concerned agree that the GTA today includes the official City of Toronto and the four surrounding regions or regional municipalities of Halton, Peel, York, and Durham. The four regions are further subdivided into an even two dozen lower-tier or area municipalities, as shown on the map (and in the table).

Some will ask whether such other nearby places as Hamilton, or Barrie, or Kitchener-Waterloo are or ought to be included in the GTA. The short answer is that they are not, or at least not yet.

Recent history does confirm that Ontario municipal geography is still subject to almost random change at the whim of provincial politicians. In 1995 there were well over 800 municipalities in Canada's most populous province. By the end of 2001 there were less than 450. Who knows where other such almost mindlessly rationalizing impulses may eventually lead? The provincial government, headquartered at Queen's Park in downtown Toronto, has now established

On the Road in the GTA

a "smart growth" panel, to report on just how well municipal public services are being provided in a mega-metropolitan region that includes the GTA and much more — to the east, north, west, and south, in a giant arc around the northwestern and just plain western shores of Lake Ontario.

Yet the present GTA — the official City of Toronto, and the surrounding four municipal regions — is as far as the term Greater Toronto can be seriously stretched at the moment, whatever any level of government may finally aspire to. And in some broader globalizing North American perspective, this Greater Toronto Area is just another version of a kind of city region (in the lexicon of Toronto's resident American urbanist, Jane Jacobs) that has sprung up in many parts of the world.

Like its older urban core, the wider GTA has a mysteriously neutral or generic quality. According to the fictional California TV character Lori Volpone, Toronto looks like every place. She was trying to explain, on the HBO show "Beggars and Choosers," why it was a good as well as an inexpensive city region in which to shoot a Hollywood TV series, whose ostensible locales ranged from Russia in the dead of winter, to the back alleys of Los Angeles in July.

The real-life Canadian author Stephen Dale has drawn related parallels between the GTA and Orange County in Southern California, in his recent book *Lost in the Suburbs*. Back in the 1970s the astutely bland Ontario premier and GTA resident, Bill Davis, liked to say that Toronto should forget about the unattainable New York model on the east coast, and see itself more realistically as a friendly rival of San Francisco, in Northern California.

In the wider North American scheme of things, Toronto is east coast or northeast obviously enough, though geographically and in other ways as well it also has a few things in common with the vast continental mid-west. Toronto is in some respects, as Peter Ustinov politely quipped in the 1980s, "New York run by the Swiss." Yet for virtually all of Canada, there is another sense again in which modern California on the Pacific coast forms a more friendly and approachable bridge to the USA today.

What Is It?

California, in certain important enough respects, is in the United States but not quite of it — as the California Republic state bear flags remind you, all over the place. In some similar ways Canada is of the United States but not quite in it, and since 1965 Canada's very vast national geography has had its own flag too. The two conditions are not identical, but they are related. And this relationship gives Toronto some things in common with both Los Angeles and San Francisco, or San Diego and San Jose, that it does not quite have with such closer places as Chicago, Detroit, Cleveland, Buffalo, Rochester, Albany, Boston, or New York.

Toronto may forever be an almost congenital emulator of New York City (along with the old imperial metropolis in London, England). But as a place in the continental urban hierarchy, it is also quite obviously much more like San Francisco — demographically, functionally, and so forth. The GTA today is still somewhat like the San Francisco Bay Area, as Bill Davis long ago suggested, without the romantic geography, the musical Spanish names, the Mediterranean climate, or quite the same high technological karma as Silicon Valley. It also has GO Transit instead of the Bay Area Rapid Transit or BART. And GO Transit has been one key for us in our discovery of the new exurbanopolis.

We ourselves are two tourists of a sort, who grew up in the older City of Toronto, as it used to be during the generation that followed the Second World War. We have visited and explored the sprawl that has subsequently arisen far beyond the old city.

At least a little like the emigrant French Canadian Jack Kerouac, in another time and place, we have gone on the road, in pursuit of what has happened to the Toronto of our youth. This is our own eclectic report on what the GTA looks and feels like today, and on at least a few of the things you might discover if you choose to explore Greater Toronto yourself.

We have concentrated on the two dozen area municipalities in the outer or "905" subregion (named after their dominant long-distance telephone code), in the regions of Halton, Peel, York, and Durham. They have as yet been much less observed than the inner or official

On the Road in the GTA

City of Toronto, but taken together they are now home to more people. Our guiding hypothesis is that they can be just as generically intriguing as the old urban core.

We have also explored a little in the present-day core itself (where the dominant long-distance telephone code is "416"). It too is a part of the GTA. It remains the strange magnet that pulls everything else together, and presents it to the world at large. Not even the most eclectic guide could altogether leave it out. In the pages that follow it appears at the very end.

A few final prefatory remarks about drawings and statistics — and GO trains and buses — may also be in order. Those who are deeply interested in such things can consult the Note on Sources and Modes of Travel at the back of the book.

Right up front it is enough to say that a short volume of this sort can only be an eclectic guide, as the subtitle says. It can only offer one quite subjective impression of the larger whole that is the GTA today. At the same time, this impression at least draws on two different clusters of private perceptions, running in more or less parallel channels. And the ultimate premise is that the end result can finally be adapted to the reader's own purposes, whatever these purposes may exactly be.

May 19, 2003.

I
Halton Region

Governor Simcoe has done a great deal for this province. He has changed the name of every place in it.

JOSEPH BRANT (Thayendanegea)

1
BURLINGTON

I f you are coming from the somewhat jaded but still compelling international tourist attraction at Niagara Falls, along the Queen Elizabeth Way, the GTA starts in the City of Burlington (just after the City of Hamilton). You will know you have landed when you descend from the James N. Allan Skyway at Burlington Beach.

Descending from the Skyway at Burlington Beach

On the sand beneath the Skyway's descent are some wood frame cottages. A few may be year-round homes that just look like cottages. But even at the start of the winter, when the place is largely abandoned, you sense that there is still some gregarious life here on hot summer nights. An apparently unofficial sign says "Hooterville."

In the same vicinity a fenced-off area of the beach is labelled "Dune Preservation Project Under Way." The project is operated by the official City of Burlington. It seems that it is not intended to preserve Hooterville too — whatever this may exactly mean. Adjacent tall hydro-electric towers along the beach nonetheless hint that the

On the Road in the GTA

place may always exude something of the old industrial culture of the steel mills, just around the bay in Hamilton.

Dune preservation project

If you walk to the east of all this, you will soon reach the old Burlington downtown. The main street, which runs north from the lake, is called Brant Street. On your way there you pass the Brant Museum and the new Brant's Landing condo project.

The street, museum, and condo project all honour the memory of Joseph Brant or Thayendanegea. He was a chief of the New York Iroquois who remained loyal to the British Crown, and moved north of the Great Lakes in the late 18th century, after the American War of Independence. Educated at a school in New England, Brant was for a brief nervous moment a well-to-do figure of consequence in the old British North American Province of Upper Canada, precursor of the present Canadian province of Ontario. His imposing house originally stood near the present-day museum.

Much more recently there was also a place called the Brant Inn, at the foot of Brant Street by the lake. It was a stomping ground for the touring big bands of North America, in the earlier and middle parts of the 20th century. A tune called the "Brant Inn Boogie" was recorded in 1948 by the Lionel Hampton Orchestra, with Wes Montgomery on guitar and Charlie Mingus on bass.

The unstoppable march of progress, and rock and roll music, eventually led to the demise of the Brant Inn. It was torn down in 1969. The foot of Brant Street, at its intersection with Lakeshore Road, is now a neater and tidier location, which just hints very vaguely at the atmosphere of several earlier eras.

Burlington

Only a short distance north, at the intersection of Brant and James streets, is today's Burlington City Hall — a good-looking structure of quite recent vintage, with some quiet smaller-scale echoes of today's city hall in downtown Toronto. A little further north on Brant Street is Upper Canada Place. Its name echoes the earlier 19th century. But it is in fact a very up-to-date downtown shopping mall.

Downtown Burlington at large today is a tidy spot, with many neat up-to-date buildings. It is rather engagingly quiet as well. The city's dynamic economic edge has a lot more to do with big trucks and newer industrial buildings in the suburbs. You start to discover this universe if you walk some distance north on Brant Street, and then turn east on Fairview, en route to the Burlington GO Transit station.

Burlington today does have its own increasingly important local economic base — and

Burlington City Hall

assorted long-standing ties to the City of Hamilton, just around what earlier generations called the head of Lake Ontario. But the cars in the GO station parking lot are a reminder that it is also still a commuter bedroom community, for people who work in the heart of the Canadian "city with the heart of loan shark," in downtown Toronto.

On the Road in the GTA

Back on the beach just west of Brant Street, near the Hooterville sign and the hydro towers, if you look east along the water on a clear enough day you can see the CN Tower and the other tall buildings in downtown Toronto — off in the distance.

A very long time ago now, during the War of 1812, some 1,400 Iroquois refugees from the Grand River Valley to the south and west, and another several hundred Shawnee warriors, had camped out on this same beach. They pitched their tents around the house of the old chief Joseph Brant, more or less in the location of the present Brant Museum. Brant himself was dead by this point, but his house was still occupied by his widow Catherine, the Metis or mixed-race daughter of the Great Lakes fur trader George Croghan and "his Indian wife." Catherine Brant was Joseph's third wife and bore him seven children. We can only wonder what she would make of the GTA today.

Hydro tower on Burlington Beach, where the Iroquois set up camp in the War of 1812

2
MILTON

If you are coming from the west along Highway 401 (from Chicago or the American motown, say), the GTA begins in the sprawling expanse of exurban landscape now rather whimsically known as the Town of Milton.

The town in its present configuration dates from as recently as 1973. Travelling west on 401 you enter it officially just east of the Mountsberg Reservoir. But it is still some distance from here before you arrive at the older built-up urban area that was once the real town of Milton.

On the way you drive by Country Heritage Park — formerly the Ontario Farm Museum. Even now downtown Milton itself has something of the feel of a 19th century agricultural service centre, from back when the family farm was everything.

Sixteen Mile Creek, winding its way through downtown Milton today

Part of this is just a greater proximity to such small natural splendours as Sixteen Mile Creek, which winds its way through the old downtown. Splendours like this give the outer reaches of the GTA one of their assorted current attractions, in a new age when too many people spend too much time with high technology at work.

Older built-up urban areas like the old town of Milton were defined by the once dominant countryside they served, not the other way around. Something similar still seems true today, even as the

On the Road in the GTA

countryside is gradually filling up with new residential subdivisions and discreet shopping malls.

The new Town of Milton includes everything: old urban area, new suburban subdivisions, more spacious exurban estate development, and surviving family farms. It has had two main incarnations over the past few decades. From the middle of the 1970s to the early 1990s its population virtually doubled, from just over 16,000 to almost 32,000 people. Then in the 1990s population growth slowed to a snail's pace, and worse. Between 1996 and 2001 Milton actually lost 633 people (figuratively speaking, of course).

Old Halton County Court House

Local politics seem to have had at least something to do with this. It is now said that installation of new piped-service infrastructure for tract housing development (i.e., water and sewers) has begun to change the picture again. And, though the GTA population at large has been booming more or less steadily for a long time, Milton has not been the only slow-growth partisan among the two dozen area municipalities beyond the City of Toronto. Yet in the more recent past it has been the only place in the GTA to go so far as losing population — a kind of extreme stress on gradualism in adapting to the progress you just can't stop.

On some related wavelength, an earlier town of Milton served as the official seat of the old Halton County. When the new Regional Municipality of Halton was created in 1973 its head office moved down south to the bigger Town of Oakville, on the Lake Ontario waterfront. The old Halton County Court House nonetheless survives as the Milton Town Hall today.

Milton

The modest but august lines of the court-house building speak for something else that has now almost altogether officially vanished. North of the Great Lakes, the world of the North American family farm in its heyday was also part of the British empire, on which the sun never set. The empire scattered a lot of quietly impressive and civilized local public buildings across Southern Ontario. They brought a few extra good manners to the rough work of carving a rugged new democracy out of the backwoods in Canada.

Not far from the court-house, the old Methodist church on Main Street wears its own memories of English churches across the sea. It also serves as a memorial to the old-time religions that helped anchor the new rural mass society of the 19th century. (Religions of all sorts are still evident in this part of the GTA, as in others. But their most striking sign in the Halton region is probably the prosperous-looking Crossroads Christian Television property, just south of Milton in the Burlington suburbs.)

Old Methodist Church on Main Street

To the north of the old town of Milton — but still in the expansive Milton of today — the Halton County Radial Railway Museum points to other long-established connections. This time they are with the spreading urban shadow of the City of Toronto, down by the water to the south and east. The museum is located "at Stop 92 on the former right-of-way of the Toronto Suburban Railway," an early 20th century precursor of the present GO Transit.

The rather new downtown Milton Mall does not share the country manners mood either. It feels more like the Eaton Centre in downtown Toronto, on a smaller scale.

Yet the great survivor in Milton today is still the continental memory of the family farm. You feel this as you pass some haphazardly stored bleachers in the Milton Fairground, at the edge of the old downtown. This is the world of baseball, Tom Sawyer, *Our Town, Picnic*, and mom and apple pie.

Bleachers at the Milton Fairground

The E.C. Drury Collegiate, and E.C. Drury School for the Hearing Impaired, on Ontario Street South, make some similar point. The names honour the memory of the leader of the province of Ontario's unique Farmer-Labour government of 1919–1923 — a now forgotten North American political brand, unknown in the old capitals of Europe (and with echoes in such neighbouring places as Michigan, Minnesota, and Wisconsin).

For a brief time after the First World War E.C. Drury was both the premier of Ontario, and the elected local member for Halton. He believed that the family farm in North America had produced the finest civilization humanity had yet seen. Something of this belief is still haunting Milton's rural-rooted municipal soul. This is one of several places in the GTA today where you can work and even think in the big city, and yet still imagine that you are living in the midst of all the old virtues, down on the farm.

3
HALTON HILLS

The simplified local government boundaries of the more recent past sometimes still echo the 19th century, which had not yet discovered how the automobile would end the tyranny of local distances. Thus Milton today has an unusually sprawling shape on the map. Both due east and due north of this shape lies the modern GTA Town of Halton Hills.

Old Georgetown railway station in Halton Hills

The town's official Internet website of the early 21st century reports that Halton Hills today "consists of three urban centres — Acton, Georgetown and the 401 Corridor — and a surrounding natural environment and rural setting where a diversity of hamlets and smaller communities offer a comfortable lifestyle and numerous opportunities for leisure activities."

The Niagara Escarpment also gives Halton Hills some particular topographical variety, though the escarpment plays a role in the adjacent towns of Milton and Caledon too. The northbound GO bus drops you off at the old Georgetown railway station: a stone structure that could be the gateway to an old-world highlands retreat.

On the Road in the GTA

Then there is what Halton Hills may now be best known for in the wider GTA. According to the radio, again and again, it is worth the drive to Acton to shop at the Olde Hide House — a big-box store specializing in stylish but still rugged leather clothing, furniture, and accessories ("We are Canada's Largest Leather Store").

Acton is in the far northwest corner of Halton Hills. Georgetown, down to the south and east, has no attraction quite like the Olde Hide House. But it is the most populous and developed part of the town today. And, unlike Milton, Halton Hills has had a growing population throughout the more recent past.

West coast house on Market Street

Migrants from outside Canada have played a role in the recent growth of Halton Hills, but not at all as much as in some other parts of the GTA. A Newfoundland memorabilia store on Main Street in Georgetown has similar goods from all of Atlantic Canada, and suggests other kinds of relatively far-flung migrants in the vicinity. An in-filled house on Market Street implies some West Coast or Vancouver influence, from the other side of the country.

At the most southeasterly beginnings of Georgetown there is a sprawling property, with the Credit River running through it, known as the Upper Canada College Outdoor Education Centre. For the moment it is still a rugged country retreat for a venerable boys' private school in the City of Toronto. And something of the school's old colonial aristocratic mood still seems to be rubbing off, even on the adjacent latest installments of suburban tract housing.

In the middle of the newer tract housing, northwest of the Upper Canada College country property, the Halton Hills Shopping Centre and the Georgetown Marketplace are the current mainstream spots for retail shopping. Further north and west, the old village of Georgetown was originally inspired by now vanished paper mills on the Credit River. The old village downtown is still not what it used to be. But it has lately been acquiring its own new leases on life. According to another local Internet website, Main Street in Georgetown today shows "a greater variety of retail and service uses than there have been for many years."

Main Street, old Georgetown, at Mill Street

Through many twists and turns, Georgetown's 19th century industrial base has similarly managed to keep up with the times. The paper mills are gone, but note such current enterprises as Neilson Dairy, Cooper Standard, BASF Canada, and Baltimore Aircoil. As matters stand, the local government planners report, "there are virtually no vacancies in the Georgetown Industrial Area ... it is anticipated that much of the new industrial growth will take place along the Halton Hills 401 industrial corridor."

On the Internet as well you can discover some of the "numerous opportunities for leisure activities" that help make Halton Hills today a compelling place to live in, even if you work outside the town. The list includes a local branch of Amnesty International, the Halton Hills

On the Road in the GTA

Aikido School, a Camera Club, a Chamber of Commerce, the Halton Hills Chapter of the Toronto Bruce Trail Club ("meet other hikers from the Halton Hills area and make new friends"), a Girls Softball Association, a Golf Academy, a Model Flying Club, a Minor Lacrosse Association, and St. John Ambulance Halton Hills.

Old house with its back on Main Street

Certain related themes are suggested by an old house that backs onto Main Street in Georgetown. It seems the kind of noble palace of the continental mid-west that the TV Munsters might like to live in. Halton Hills also has late 19th century architecture that has been well-maintained and even carefully renovated. (A high school designed by the "prominent Toronto architect Edward Lennox" is one example.) Yet it has also left room for places in which some of the real ghosts from its past might feel more at home.

Meanwhile there is the future to worry about. On the Internet you can discover an organization known as Halton Hills Fibre Optics, pointing to the newest railways and highways of the present age. And the Olde Hide House in Acton has recently opened a new superstore, on King Street West in downtown Toronto.

4
OAKVILLE

If you keep going south from Halton Hills on the old 9th Line, you will finally wind up on Ford Drive, in the Town of Oakville.

The south end of Ford Drive empties onto Lakeshore Road — a long east-west thoroughfare that starts in Burlington and follows the Lake Ontario waterfront, through Oakville and Mississauga, all the way to the east end of the old city of Toronto.

Lake Ontario shoreline in Oakville

The long reach of this waterfront street is just one reflection of how the northwestern shore of Lake Ontario anchors the Greater Toronto Area. For a time in the 1970s Queen's Park planners wanted to call the emerging wider Toronto region the Central Ontario Lakeshore Urban Complex. The concept proved quite unable to fly in the real world. (Who would want to buy a new house in COLUC?) But the name was apt in some respects.

According to archaeologists, human history on this lakeshore began more than 10,000 years ago. Oakville as we know it today only dates back to 1827, when the local magnate William Chisholm purchased 960 acres of crown land (earlier purchased by the Crown from the Mississauga branch of the aboriginal peoples of Canada), in the flat area where Sixteen Mile Creek empties into the lake. Now the area is just a large dot on a much vaster municipal shoreline, stretching from east of Joshua's Creek to a point west of Twelve Mile Creek.

House of William Moulds, Trafalgar Road

According to some interpretations, Oakville today is the jewel of Halton region — or even the entire GTA. Part of this flows from a number of surviving buildings in the area of William Chisholm's original 19th century village. They have been remarkably well-preserved and maintained. The men who built them have also been documented by local history authors David and Suzanne Peacock.

You can reach these heritage structures easily from the main Oakville GO station, by taking a short walk east to Trafalgar Road and then proceeding south. Along the way, at 373 Trafalgar, you will pass what was originally the house of "William Moulds, Carpenter," erected in 1857. Moulds appears as well on the lists of artisans at the end of the Peacocks' book, *Old Oakville: A character study of the town's early buildings and of the men who built them.*

The Peacocks stress that Moulds and his colleagues were just ordinary tradesmen of their time and place. The buildings they erected, from the 1830s to the 1890s, very broadly followed the big 19th century progression of architectural styles. But the styles were rarely "represented in their purest form." It is best to "accept them as vernacular adaptations of the classical modes." Even so, carpenters like William Moulds built very solid structures, with a passion for the arts and crafts of their trades. That so many of their buildings are still standing, in such nicely maintained condition, tells how their tradition of doing ordinary things carefully and well lives on.

Oakville, the automobile city: Bronte and Lakeshore roads

Oakville today is of course not much closer to perfection than any place else. Though it is still called a town, it is in fact a suburban "edge city" of close to 150,000 people, sprawling far beyond the 19th century village, and passionately wedded to the automobile. Yet even the latest smart regiments of tract housing, to the east and north and west, have some reputation for high quality — in new subdivision neighbourhoods with such names as Glen Abbey and River Oaks.

The contemporary automobile city is also home to Ford Canada's head offices, and rather tidy-looking van and truck assembly plants, just west of Ford Drive. But Ford Canada is not native to Oakville. It moved in the 1950s from Windsor, Ontario (just across the river from Detroit). Since then even its heritage of smokestack manufacturing has somehow been locally gentrified by the artisan traditions of William Moulds.

Oakville, in any case, remains a near-exact opposite of a smokestack town. In 1996 it had the highest percentage of university graduates in the GTA. In 2001 it had the highest percentage of immigrants from outside Canada in Halton region (almost 28%). It is a place

On the Road in the GTA

where people hold sparkling June weddings in vast backyards — a sprawling suburb where even the strip malls have some distinction.

Street repairs on Bronte Road

Some distance from William Chisholm's 19th century village, the Bronte GO station in today's west-end Oakville is surrounded by a resolutely up-to-date industrial area, just south of the Queen Elizabeth Way. If you walk west from the station on Wyecroft Road, however, you will eventually land at Bronte Road. From here you can take another southbound journey down to the lake.

In the fall of 2001 there are street repairs in progress on Bronte Road. But this street follows Twelve Mile Creek to the waterfront, much as Trafalgar Road to the east follows Sixteen Mile Creek. Even under repair it has some minor magic (as in the house of folk artist James Paterson, surrounded by some of his satirical creations).

It is no doubt possible to be too proud of old buildings. Yet on a sunny autumn afternoon this seems almost entirely beside the point. Bronte Road ends at a long pier that stretches out into the lake. Immediately west rests the present-day fleet of the Bronte Harbour Yacht Club. In an earlier day Bronte was a hamlet unto itself. The yacht club reminds you that it does belong in Oakville. It too is part of the jewel of the Halton region, or even the entire GTA.

II
Peel Region

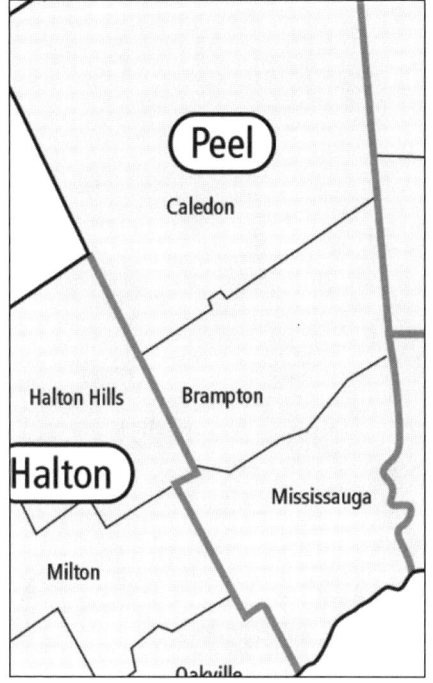

Cars in parking lot, Mississauga City Centre

5
MISSISSAUGA

Due east of Oakville along the waterfront lies the City of Mississauga. With its own stretch of Lakeshore Road, it is the currently reluctant anchor of the parsimonious wider region of Peel, which has only three constituent parts: Mississauga in the south, Brampton in the middle, and Caledon in the north.

With 612,925 inhabitants in the 2001 Canadian federal census, Mississauga is also by far the most populous of the two dozen 905 area municipalities in the GTA — and the closest demographic rival of the present-day City of Toronto. Not surprisingly, it is also due west of the city proper. In an earlier incarnation it was actually known as Toronto Township.

The historian David Gagan has shown that even in its earlier days as Toronto Township, in the middle of the 19th century, the mood of this particular chunk of geography had a lot in common with its mood today. Then as now, it was full of *Hopeful Travellers* (as Gagan called his book on the subject) — great masses of ambitious people from various old and new parts of the world, restless to get ahead.

Then carving a family farm out of the wilderness was the main road to success. Now it is doing some demanding enough skilled or professional job for the almost unfathomable number of large and small goods- and service-producing corporations in the GTA — or perhaps running your own related small business.

In some respects, the endless tracts of brand new and still-not-very-old suburban housing have just carried on the old symmetrical geography and even some of the culture of the family farm, at a much denser level of landscape development. And in some ways too even the new and almost desperately functional suburban high-rise apartment and office buildings, especially clustered by the Mississauga City Centre, just take the same trend to some nth degree.

From another angle again, the local tradition of hopeful travelling itself predates the rise of the 19th century family farm. The present-day name Mississauga replaced Toronto Township in 1968, as the result of a local referendum. It honours the memory of the particular branch of the aboriginal peoples of Canada who were living in the area when the 19th century began. But in fact the Mississauga were not native to the place themselves. They had only arrived by the early 18th century, as victors of a sort in the wake of various fur-trade conflicts or "beaver wars," induced by the early rumblings of an expanding world economy in the North American Great Lakes.

Schoolchildren at the Living Arts Centre

However far back into the past you look, what you have in Mississauga today certainly is acres and acres of late 20th century North American suburban tract housing. Torontonians who visit Southern California report back that it looks a lot like Mississauga. Or, more exactly, Mississauga looks a lot like the endless suburbs around Los Angeles, mere climate and physical geography aside.

For a quarter of a century modern Mississauga has been shrewdly guided by Mayor Hazel McCallion — a tough local lady with roots in the earlier Toronto Township village of Streetsville. In the late spring of 2003 she is 82 years old and still vigorously in office.

Under Mayor McCallion, the new city has made some serious effort to breathe an older kind of local civic life into present-day suburbia. One focus of this effort has been the carefully planned new downtown at the Mississauga City Centre, anchored by the Square One shopping mall. With due allowances for what has been possible in the real world of politics, the City Centre is sort of located in the middle of Mississauga's municipal geography, right off Highway 403, which at this juncture strategically connects Highway 401 to the north with the Queen Elizabeth Way to the south.

Mississauga

If your idea of a downtown is still passionately wedded to the pedestrian-friendly 19th century streetscape in the old downtown of the City of Toronto, you may not be altogether impressed by the new suburban downtown at the Mississauga City Centre.

Some key public facilities are concentrated in the area, along with the mall at Square One — the city hall, the main library branch, the Living Arts Centre, an Art Gallery, some office buildings, and a YMCA. But if you explore the place on foot you will be struck by how spread out everything is. This is the universe according to the mind of the automobile traffic engineer. As a pedestrian, you keep coming back to the barren feeling which haunts too much of the inhumanly vast open space in suburbia.

Pedestrians on Burnhamthorpe Road

On the other hand, the Mississauga City Centre is clearly trying to do something constructive, and it is a lot more elegant than a strip mall. The new city hall has some up-to-date architectural distinction. The fittings inside say something about all the new wealth that has quietly assembled in the area over the past several decades. Some complain that the Living Arts Centre is underused by the general public. But it is no doubt expanding the minds of large numbers of schoolchildren, happy enough to visit in groups, instead of sitting in their classrooms.

The main branch of the public library is impressive as well. There are quite a few people there, even in the middle of the week. And the bookshelves exude their own cosmopolitan urbanity. Like the City of Toronto proper next door, the City of Mississauga in the early 21st century is a place of quite stupendous cultural diversity.

In 2001 just under 47% of Mississauga's population was born outside Canada. The area has been a recurrent gathering place for recent immigrants for centuries. Nowadays they come from around the world. Wandering by the shelves at the main branch of the public library you can see books and magazines in Urdu, Vietnamese, Spanish, Tagalog, Tamil, Ukrainian, Portuguese, Punjabi, Russian, Serbian, Japanese, Korean, Polish, Italian, Hungarian, Gujurati, Hindi, German, Greek, and on and on and on.

Who knows? Maybe there will be different genres of urbanity in the future of the exurbanopolis. Even now, the main thrust of Mississauga isn't just the City Centre, surrounded by endless acres of suburban tract housing. It also includes an assortment of villages and hamlets from the earlier family farm heydays of Toronto Township.

There are still distinct vestiges, for example, of Streetsville on the upper reaches of Mullett Creek, Port Credit at the mouth of the Credit River, on Lake Ontario, Clarkson (also on the lake), Cooksville on what is now the Queen Elizabeth Way, and Malton in the northeast corner of Mississauga today.

Malton was once home to rather extensive aircraft manufacturing facilities of A.V. Roe Canada Ltd. Now it is host to the main air traffic centre for all of the GTA, at Lester B. Pearson International Airport — currently operated by "a corporation without share capital" called the Greater Toronto Airports Authority, or GTAA.

The GTAA has a board of directors appointed by the City of Toronto, the regional municipalities of Halton, Peel, York, and Durham, the Province of Ontario, and the Government of Canada. Its chief executive officer in the winter of 2002–2003 is Louis A. Turpen, who "served for 14 years as Director of the San Francisco International Airport."

Mississauga

Mississauga City Hall

The 19th and earlier 20th century villages and hamlets have been focal points for somewhat more diverse forms of suburban development, that help relieve the monotony of the tract housing in the new city of the 21st century. Some of the tract houses themselves have wonderful gardens, unusual outdoor lighting systems, recreational welding shops in basements, intriguing prefabricated backyard sheds, and rocks from Muskoka on their front lawns.

In the mall at Square One

Mississauga today has public parks along the Credit River. The Rattray Marsh Conservation Area, at the edge of Lake Ontario, is a fine place for Sunday walks in almost any weather. There are suburban Chinatowns, many restaurants, local jazz festivals, and a regional campus of the University of Toronto. Mayor McCallion — more vigorous in her early eighties most of us in our fifties (or much younger still) — is the undoubted lion in winter of municipal politics in all of the GTA, including the City of Toronto proper.

So say what you like. At this point in history Mississauga does seem to be the kind of new city that a lot of people want.

6
BRAMPTON

The City of Brampton, due north of Mississauga, is the second most populous 905 municipality in the GTA today. It is also the almost historic home of Bill Davis — who said "bland works" in Ontario politics, and then proved it by remaining premier of the province for more than 14 years, from 1971 to 1985.

When bland still worked ... older housing on the edge of the downtown

Bland may not work so well anymore. Brampton's most glamourous recent distinction, as global headquarters for the high-tech multinational Nortel Networks, was profoundly tarnished by the global dot.com crash. But there is still a lot of diverse new life in this once sliced-white-bread industrial city, which has started to become who knows just what.

Among the latest additions to the place is a growing South Asian population — new empire loyalists of a sort, from the old British Raj on the Indian subcontinent. Officially sanctioned statuary on the grounds of the tidy city hall downtown elaborates on the theme. It shows three teenage girls dancing, with their hands joined, in a circle: one is Asian, one is black, and one is Caucasian.

On the Road in the GTA

In 2001 immigrants born outside Canada accounted for 40% of the wider local population. This puts Brampton somewhat behind Mississauga to the south, and Markham, Richmond Hill, and Vaughan in York region to the east as well. But it is still well ahead of all other GTA municipalities outside the City of Toronto itself — to say nothing of Ontario (27% immigrant), Canada (18%), or the USA (12%) at large.

*Three girls dancing
Brampton City Hall*

Just south of the city hall, at Queen and Main streets downtown, is the quite nostalgic Gage Park. It includes a still nicely maintained municipal bandstand. In days gone by such structures hosted concerts in the park by the marching bands of local militia regiments. Just around the corner today, on Queen Street, an old red-brick building bears a sign which suggests some of the changing tastes afoot: the BRAMPTON CONCERT BAND, the JAZZ MECHANICS.

Mechanics more generally is an interesting term here, with another variety of local relevance. Back in the 19th century the Brampton area was part of the universe that warmed to the continental rhetoric of the free and democratic "farmers and mechanics," who helped make Abraham Lincoln president of the USA. (In Canada a more sober local variation on the theme was promoted by the upright Scottish immigrant and Toronto press baron George Brown, founder of what is now known as the *Globe and Mail*.)

Mechanics of other sorts again still figure prominently in the local labour force. The Nortel Networks global headquarters, on Dixie Road some distance south and east of the bandstand in Gage

Brampton

Park, does not imply that Brampton is a place haunted by groves of academe. In 1996 less than 15% of the city's population 25 years of age and over had completed university — compared with more than 30% in the upscale GTA towns of Oakville and Markham.

*Nortel Networks global headquarters
Dixie Road*

Brampton today is still a version of the prosperous smaller industrial city that especially came together during its more recent 20th century past. It is still providing the opportunities such places can still provide, for many different kinds of people who are not afraid of hard work. The actual Nortel Networks building on Dixie Road fits in, somehow. It is not easy to say just what it looks like. But it doesn't

Affordable housing, just northwest of Nortel

quite look like the headquarters of a high-tech multinational corporation. Much of the new exurban suburbia that has also arisen some distance from the old Brampton downtown fits in some similar way as well. Back in the late 1960s and early 1970s, the Bramalea development, in the east end of the present city, became a hotbed of affordable new housing for hard-working Torontonians, new and old alike.

If you walk through what the subsequent decades have wrought, on the route from Gage Park to Dixie Road, you probably won't be struck by sublime thoughts. But you might imagine that a realistic person nowadays could do a lot worse than Brampton in the GTA.

The former Ontario premier Bill Davis still ranks as the city's most celebrated resident of the recent past. He was almost agonizingly bland. But he did seem to believe in something decent. He thought the future was worth getting ready for. And he had a comfortably rumpled but orderly and even tidy exterior. Something similar still seems stuck to the early 21st century pavement in Brampton. Just what will finally become of it does remain unknown.

7
CALEDON

Due north of Brampton lies the Town of Caledon. Here, on some cusp between the regions of Peel and York, the traveller who started on Burlington Beach enters a new kind of ubiquitous GTA countryside.

Coming into the old village of Caledon from the west, on the Charleston or 15th Sideroad

Both Milton and Halton Hills, in the Halton region to the west, are in the countryside too, in several senses. But each also enjoys at least one old urban centre of real demographic weight, around which the newest exurban development can vaguely focus. Present-day Caledon has no such place.

Here the rural landscape invented in the 19th century is relieved strictly by smaller old villages, hamlets, and crossroads churches and general stores — Albion, Alton, Bolton, Boston Mills, Caledon East, Caledon village, Cedar Mills, Inglewood, Mono Road, Palgrave, Sandhill, Terra Cotta, and so forth.

Yet here too you are still in Peel region, very close to the biggest demographic heavyweight in the City of Toronto. In 2001 the Town of Caledon had a larger population than either Milton or Halton Hills. It can claim some distinction as that part of the current exurban sprawl where the largest number of people have sprawled the most.

The Tack Shop on Hurontario Street

Caledon today can claim assorted other distinctions as well. It has the highest average income in Peel region — higher than either Brampton or Mississauga. One implication is that there are residents who can afford to keep horses, not so much because they think the horses will somehow prove useful, but just because they like horses (still the great heritage transportation mode of the 19th century, railways notwithstanding). On Hurontario Street, in the old village of Caledon, there is the In the Ribbons Equestrian Store, attached to a place with a sign that says Tack Shop, and right next door to Wooden Bucket Antiques and Country Gifts.

On some similar trajectory, the Town of Caledon can also boast a few especially distinguished human residents. The Toronto-born Hollywood movie director Norman Jewison maintains a 280-acre farm here, which raises prize Hereford cattle. A gentleman called Jim apparently manages the farm, but it is reported that Jewison helps bring in the hay every year. John Roth, the former chief executive officer of the beleaguered Nortel Networks, was born and raised in Montreal, but now has a country estate in Caledon in Greater Toronto. The late great Canadian novelist Robertson Davies also kept a Caledon residence, and the hamlet of Boston Mills has given its name to a noted Canadian small-press publisher.

Almost hidden tract housing around Mistywood Park

At the same time, it would be wrong to imply that Caledon today is all about high culture and high income. The real countryside is more diverse and eclectic. The average income is not so high as in Oakville to the south and west. There are almost ramshackle country buildings here and there. On Hurontario Street just south of the Tack Shop and Equestrian Store is Eddie Shack Donuts, trading on the name of a defiantly lowbrow old Toronto Maple Leafs hockey star.

Like Mississauga and Brampton in Peel region, Caledon can similarly boast its own more conventional patches of new suburban tract housing, especially in Bolton but in other places as well. Yet even here the countryside tends to be more ubiquitous than in some other parts of the wider region. The tract housing is sometimes almost hidden by trees and bushes and related signs of nature. It seems to intrude less on the wide-open feeling you get as you travel around.

There are a few industrial subdivisions in Caledon today too. But in the very end the ubiquitous countryside continues to settle down on the farm. Bill Davis liked to explain that there were still some farmers even in the City of Brampton in the 1970s. In the early 21st century there are certainly still some farmers in the Town of Caledon.

Farm gate on Charleston Sideroad

Just how much altogether economically serious agricultural activity goes on is a question for agricultural experts. They sometimes seem to be telling us that there is not all that much activity of this sort going on nowadays in the entire province of Ontario. But a July 2002 report from the Town of Caledon planning staff urges that there is still some good agricultural land in the municipality, which constitutes a "resource worth protecting," especially on the more southerly Peel Plain. Further meetings with "stakeholders" in the resource are being held, "consistent with the perceived image of Caledon as an authentic 'slice of rural Ontario Countryside.'"

Meanwhile, early 21st century country life in the North American exurbs continues — still drenched in legends of the old family farm, and increasingly haunted by more remote second-hand memories of still older landed gentries, across assorted seas.

III
York Region

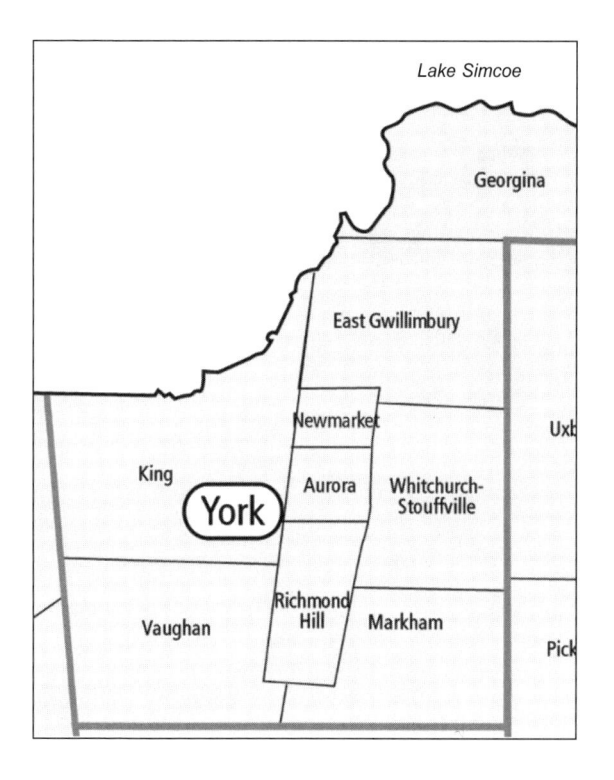

Sawn logs, just northwest of the King City GO station

8
KING

Just east of Caledon is the Township of King — or as its best-known highway intersection is quite whimsically called, King City. Officially, when you move from Caledon to King you have also moved from Peel region to the region of York. Unofficially, King Township extends the same ubiquitous countryside that the Town of Caledon has already introduced.

On an alternate route, there is a northbound GO bus to King City from Union Station in downtown Toronto. It drops you off at the intersection of Keele Street and Station Road.

Just a stone's throw west from the bus stop an old line of tracks from Toronto, originally known as the Ontario, Simcoe & Huron Railway, runs more or less parallel with Keele Street. Station Road leads to today's GO rail station. In the morning this is also the point of departure for the southbound commuter rail traffic to the big city. Even in this direction, however, there can't be too many people involved: a small Plexiglas shelter serves as the GO station building.

To confirm that you have indeed landed in an exotic countryside, just northwest of the GO rail station stands some species of updated rural sawmill, surrounded by neat stacks of freshly cut logs. But if you go back out to Keele Street and walk north you will soon be in downtown King City, at the intersection of Keele and the King Sideroad. Here there are some residences and a few commercial buildings — including several very nicely maintained heritage properties, with origins in the 19th century.

A small solid-brick Baptist chapel, around the corner on the King Sideroad, bears the date 1873. Back on the east side of Keele Street an immaculate old wood-frame building, freshly painted in a blue-grey tone with fastidious white trim, has a sign over the front porch: Crawford Wells General Store Ltd. What you get inside, however, is more like an upscale modern card and gift boutique.

Walking east along the north side of the King Sideroad, you might soon enough find yourself in a very up-to-date Country Style Donuts outlet. At noon it fills with teenagers from the high school, down the road a little more.

On the Road in the GTA

These young people have easy access to such places as the valley of the East Humber River, west of Keele Street and north of the King Sideroad. Though the river at this point is little more than a creek, you can still feel lost in nature standing beside it. You can still hear the cars and trucks on Keele Street too.

Back at the downtown crossroads, you can look west and see the King Sideroad following a bridge across the railway tracks, and then stretching off into a still sprawling countryside. The view is a reminder that King City is not all of King Township. There are similar exotic crossroad places off to the west and north, with names like Nobleton, Pottageville, Lloydtown, and Schomberg.

General store in King City

Not far north of the King Sideroad, Keele Street hosts a very large Gilbert and Sullivan country estate, built in the late 1930s by the Eaton family — Toronto-based moguls of a now defunct Canada-wide chain of department stores. Life on this scale in the modern age can be fleeting, and the romance of Eaton Hall did not last long. Since 1971 the place has served as the suburban King Campus of Seneca College of Applied Arts and Technology (whose main campus is to the south, in the old City of Scarborough which is now part of the new City of Toronto).

Perhaps as some memorial to the earlier splendour of Eaton Hall, King Township at large now has the highest average income in the entire GTA. It also has one of the smallest populations, and the immediate evidence is that this will not be changing any time soon. Between 1996 and 2001 a mere 310 people were added to the total township numbers — another Greater Toronto case of unbridled political passions for very slow growth.

The King Sideroad, looking west across the railway tracks

Some would stress that the politics involved are not just local. King Township, the story goes, still lacks the public piped-service infrastructure to support dense tract-housing development. Building it would wreak ecological havoc with the surrounding natural heritage of the Oak Ridges Moraine. And the preservation of the moraine is now said to be an article of faith, among even the most revolutionary libertarian strains of partisan opinion, throughout the GTA.

As things stand, living in King Township today is a limited option for several different regional minorities. They include certain sorts of quite rich people, some of whom, as in the neighbouring and much more populous Town of Caledon, own horses. They also include refugees from the culture wars of the 1960s, some rural or perhaps "rurban" people with authentically deep roots in the area, and various small minority branches of the big-city managerial class who really do want to live in the country. All these people together add up to the township's current population of less than 20,000.

If these people have their way, their club will be taking on only a few new members each year. There will be no rapid growth in this part of the GTA any time soon.

Some King residents will point out that this does not imply any seriously exclusive enclave. For a still essentially rural municipality of its relative demographic weight, the township does have an unusually high percentage of immigrants in its current population (21% in the 2001 census). As in other GTA municipalities further away from the City of Toronto, there has been some modest stalling in this trend lately. But there has also been an acceleration in the growth of immigrant populations closer to the big city, and this suggests that the stalling further away cannot last forever.

Heritage housing on Keele Street King Township

Who can hope to predict the future of such things in the still quite new and mysterious 21st century? Meanwhile, again, life in the exotic countryside goes on. But it is not quite as it was in days gone by. You feel this when you look at the nicely maintained heritage housing in downtown King City. (As old as they are, these buildings probably never looked this good before.) And you feel it still more on a sunny summer afternoon, sitting out on the patio of the Greek restaurant on Keele Street, sipping white wine, watching the rurban gentry go about their business, in rather expensive cars and trucks.

9
EAST GWILLIMBURY

If you drive up into the northeast corner of King Township, along Dufferin Street, and then turn east on the Graham Sideroad, you will soon enough find yourself in the Town of East Gwillimbury. Here the ubiquitous exurban countryside just carries on, with some local variations of its own.

Sharon Temple, on Leslie Street

To start with, there is the Sharon Temple, built over a seven-year period, from 1825 to 1831, to serve a local religious group called the Children of Peace. The group was the invention of David Wilson, who had earlier emigrated to East Gwillimbury from New York State, with his wife and children and some relatives and neighbours.

Wilson was an ardently individualistic frontier family farmer of deep convictions. In East Gwillimbury he at first attached himself to some local Quakers. Then he quarrelled with them about music, among other things, and formed the Children of Peace. This attracted enough followers in the immediate vicinity to erect the house of worship that still stands today on Leslie Street, in the old village of

Sharon. It is a square wood-frame structure with lots of windows, in three narrowing and ascending layers, symbolizing the Holy Trinity of the Christian faith.

Town of East Gwillimbury Civic Centre (viewed from the rear)

After David Wilson's death in the mid-1860s, the Children of Peace gradually dispersed. The fate of the Sharon Temple remained uncertain for some time. Then, in the earlier 20th century, the York Pioneer & Historical Society took on the task of preserving its unique architectural heritage. The building stands today in a well-maintained condition — a memorial to some quality in the lives of Wilson and his followers that must have been meant to last.

You might also guess that the Children of Peace have somehow prompted the much more recently erected municipal offices of the Town of East Gwillimbury, just north of the Sharon Temple on Leslie Street. As the firebrand journalist William Lyon Mackenzie said of the temple in its day, this late 20th century building seems "calculated to inspire the beholder with astonishment." Opinions about its architecture vary. But on any view it is quite unlike the usual local government offices for a municipality of some 20,000 people.

East Gwillimbury

The Children of Peace were prosperous 19th century family farmers, and something of this legacy is still close to the surface in East Gwillimbury. The main centres of recent exurban population growth are the old villages of Holland Landing (on the Holland River), Mount Albert, Queensville, and Sharon. But in between these places you can still walk by some obviously working family farms.

Farm machinery on Leslie Street

Judging by the names on the mail boxes, these farms are now often enough quite large enterprises, occupying parents and children and brothers and sisters alike, on adjacent parcels of land. Farm machinery is now altogether crucial, and there are places where you can purchase it or get it repaired.

Yet here once again life in the countryside is not what it used to be. If you walk along Leslie Street from Sharon to Queensville between 5 and 6 PM on a weekday, you get the strange sensation of being in both an old rural countryside and new urban rush-hour traffic at once. There are a lot of northbound automobiles racing past the cornfields, and the strip-ribbon houses in between the farms.

In the late summer and fall, Vince's Country Market in Sharon has fresher corn and other produce than you usually get in the biggest city to the south. It is otherwise much like supermarkets you can find even in the depths of downtown Toronto. In Queensville there is a general store that, from the outside, still has something of the nostalgic country manners mood from gentler days gone by. Inside, it just seems like a conventional urban or suburban convenience store — a kind of 7 Eleven, in a building that is showing its age.

Queensville General Store

East Gwillimbury has a few more people than neighbouring King Township today. Its average income is not notably low, but it is not all that notably high either. Just a little north of the Sharon Temple, on the other side of Leslie Street, there is a Kingdom Hall of Jehovah's Witnesses. It suggests one modern direction in which some of the legacies of the Children of Peace have gone.

Other still more up-to-date legacies are flowing from the same old spring. In the hot late summer of 2002 the earlier villages of Holland Landing, Mount Albert, and Queensville have their own Internet websites. A website for Sharon is "under construction." Already on the website for the Sharon Temple you can take a virtual walking tour of a number of 19th century buildings in Sharon. Some of them are dwellings where the Children of Peace once lived. Almost 140 years after his death, in this part of the new exurbanoplis David Wilson is still making some waves.

10
GEORGINA

Continuing north on Leslie Street in East Gwillimbury will eventually take you into the almost exotically eclectic Town of Georgina. Its key geographic feature is that it stretches to the northerly limits of the GTA on the shores of Lake Simcoe. During the long hot summer of 2002, it also seems a place of deeper human undercurrents than you might guess from a map.

Looking north onto Lake Simcoe from the Town of Georgina

The first point about the exurban countryside here is that it marks the most southerly beginnings of the old Toronto cottage country. Its growth in the late 19th and early 20th centuries was an earlier stage in the urban invasion that has finally led to the GTA in the late 20th and early 21st centuries. In the right season you can still catch strong murmurs of the holiday mood almost as soon as you cross from East Gwillimbury into Georgina — at Miami Beach, Elmhurst Beach, Beegalo Beach, and Keswick, on Cook's Bay.

Nowadays, Keswick is also the site of new year-round condominiums by the waterfront. Some of them are occupied by people who drive to jobs in downtown Toronto every weekday. Elsewhere as well, following east along the main shoreline of Lake Simcoe, yesterday's near vacation land is in transition.

The Red Barn Theatre today

Jackson's Point, more or less in the middle of Georgina's northern shoreline, was once a big attraction for urbane Torontonians. From 1907 to 1948 a radial railway directly linked it to the old city. After this closed, in 1949, Alfred Mulock and his wife, actress Teffi Lock, started the Red Barn Theatre, in a building originally erected in 1876. The Red Barn survives down to the present as "Canada's oldest summer stock theatre." The 2002 season included five different shows, appearing in sequence from June 6 to September 14.

Other echoes of older salad days live on in some remaining upscale properties by the lake. But the most striking thing about Jackson's Point today is the sleepy and even somewhat abandoned state of its commercial core — especially in the middle of the week. There are old cottage properties that now seem abandoned as well, and some new condo projects which are not quite finished.

There are also other senses in which the present Town of Georgina provides a retreat from life in the big city. It has almost twice as many people as East Gwillimbury — along with the second-lowest average income in the GTA (after the Township of Brock due east), and the smallest percentage of university graduates (just over 8% in 1996). Here there are still quite a few people who, as they say, work to live, rather than live to work as they do downtown.

Old store waiting for something new to happen, Lake Drive, Jackson's Point

Just south and east of Jackson's Point, on the outskirts of Sutton, is the related Sutton-by-the-Lake retirement community — a variation on the suburban tract housing theme, involving theoretically movable modular houses on smallish parcels of rented land.

South of Lake Simcoe, inland, other older villages and hamlets are still adding their own eclectic variety to life in Georgina — Baldwin, Belhaven, Cedarbrae, Egypt, Mount Pleasant, Pefferlaw, and Virginia. (Egypt, however, is certainly the sort of place you will miss if you blink driving through). Back up at the waterfront, just east of Jackson's Point, Sibbald Point Provincial Park honours the memory of people who played a prominent role in the area's 19th century development, and even erected the original Red Barn.

The Sibbalds were a Scottish family of British military officers who, among other things, built the first Anglican church in the vicinity. Mrs. Susan Sibbald from Scotland, wife of Colonel Sibbald, first came to the shores of Lake Simcoe in 1835. She had become alarmed when two of her young sons wrote to tell her that they were lodging at a local tavern. In 2002 all of the upscale and downscale and in-between sides of the Town of Georgina still seem to come together at a similar new establishment called the Lake Simcoe Arms, a stone's throw from the GO bus stop at Jackson's Point.

You can get a decent lunch at the Lake Simcoe Arms nowadays, even on a weekday in the middle of the summer. The place occupies a renovated small hotel from the 19th century. In its present incarnation it was established as recently as the year 2000, by a former general manager of the King Edward Hotel in Toronto and his son. The son is a graduate of the hospitality program at Ryerson University downtown.

The Lake Simcoe Arms in Georgina today (where something new has already happened)

In another kind of homage to the Sibbald family, the food leans towards old-country pub fare ("Enjoy a Taste of Britain"). On draught are such UK brands as Guinness Stout, Smithwick's, and Tetley's English Ale. But you can also obtain more domestic fare: Molson Canadian, Coor's Light, Rickard's Red, and Algonquin Honey Brown. The "cheque average is $12.00 for lunch and $19.00 for dinner." You walk away feeling that the Town of Georgina still has a future, as well as a past.

11
WHITCHURCH-STOUFFVILLE

If you follow Highway 48 south out of Sutton, in the Town of Georgina, you will soon be back in East Gwillimbury. But if you keep driving south you will finally land at the Town of Whitchurch-Stouffville (pronounced "Stow-vill") — the last of York region's four big municipalities in the ubiquitous exurban countryside. Whitchurch-Stouffville's official motto is "Country Close to the City," and it is another kind of transitional zone in its own right.

There are a few stark similarities with King Township back to the west, on the other side of the Yonge Street corridor. Whitchurch-Stouffville has the second-highest average income in the GTA. According to the official town website it also has "1,640 horses on 127 properties and 619 riders ... one of the largest concentrations of horses in Canada."

There are enough horses here to form a small village of their own. But the Stouffville part of the hyphenated name points to a real old village with even larger

New buildings on Main Street in old Stouffville (and note Canadian flag)

numbers of human beings, in the southeast corner of the municipality. This gives the country close to the city a stronger focus for new tract housing than any comparable centre in King. Whitchurch-Stouffville also has a somewhat larger population than King

Township, and it has grown at a mildly more rapid pace over the past several decades.

Some of Whitchurch-Stouffville's connections with the big city and its surroundings have a long history. As the official website explains, most of the municipality "is located on the Oak Ridges Moraine ... an immense geological feature formed by glacial action 14,000 years ago." Four less ancient water transportation routes in the wider region originate from the moraine here — "the Rouge River and Duffins Creek which flow south and the Holland and Black Rivers which flow to the north."

Railway line just north of the GO station

Nowadays three southbound GO trains leave the Stouffville station every weekday morning, for those who regularly connect with jobs downtown. They are a more up-to-date alternative to aboriginal canoes on the Rouge River, for reaching the Lake Ontario waterfront.

It says something about Whitchurch-Stouffville as well that it has such a technically apt official motto as Country Close to the City. (The website for the Township of King just says "Welcome Home.") The town website is similarly distinguished by a concise and rather rigorous account of the local past, since the first modern survey of old Whitchurch Township in the early 1800s.

The 200-acre farm lots of the old township are the fundamental point of departure for the present-day Town of Whitchurch-

Whitchurch-Stouffville

Stouffville, established in 1971. In the wake of the mid-19th century railway age, the old village of Stouffville (named after Abraham Stouffer, who had moved from Pennsylvania in 1804) was officially separated from the township and incorporated in its own right, in 1877. Some 95 years later, in the wake of the 20th century age of the automobile, the old village and township were legally reunited, along with such smaller urban hamlets as Bethesda, Cedar Valley, Churchill, Lincolnville, Pleasantville, and Preston Lake.

At the same time, the Yonge Street corridor centres of Newmarket and Aurora also had earlier ties to old Whitchurch Township. But they have gone on to more narrowly focused urban destinies. Whitchurch-Stouffville today is close to the city, but still mainly a part of the country.

On a sunny morning in the late spring of 2001 you can see this even in the heart of old Stouffville, where the well-maintained heritage housing still exudes its own country gentility: close to the big city but a lot more peaceful. As if to stress the point, town daughters who seem to have been raised on milk and honey are painting the Main Street fire hydrants in bright colours.

Heritage housing in Whitchurch-Stouffville

There are some quite new commercial buildings on Main Street too, and lots of Canadian flags. It is not surprising that the present town with a hyphenated name has its own coat of arms, designed by International Coats of Arms, Heraldic House Limited, and "officially adopted ... on November 27, 1973." Yet the rural areas north of

Toronto were also fertile ground for supporters of the Upper Canadian Rebellion of 1837. According to local journalist Jim Thomas, Whitchurch-Stouffville today is "definitely the Flag Capital of Canada ... Even visitors from south of the border, always enthusiastic flag-wavers, have commented on the incredible number of maple leaf banners," in all corners of the municipality.

At the back of the IGA on Main Street

Almost as if to sum everything up, there is classical music playing at a coffee and bagel shop, in a newer building on Main Street (even Mozart, maybe). Two older gentlemen are sitting by the window in the morning sun. They have nice manners, but faces which once spent a lot of time outdoors. In their prime they may have been happiest delivering produce to the Independent Grocers' Association store across the street. Now they are part of their own new leisure class. Perhaps they have quite profitably sold most of their farm land to some real estate developer — and perhaps they are actually aware that someone with a notebook is listening right now.

"Nice music, eh?" the one says to the other, with a smile.

"Yeah," the other says: "Do you wanna dance?"

12
NEWMARKET

When you move west from the northwest corner of Whitchurch-Stouffville, into the Town of Newmarket, you enter a new universe in York region. Nowadays this is the bustling zone of the exurban north Yonge Street corridor — the near countryside extension of the City of Toronto's main street.

The dam on the Holland River, Water Street, Newmarket

Back in the mists of time, Yonge Street was just how early British colonial officials tried to modernize the Toronto Passage. And the Passage was an aboriginal canoe and portage route from Lake Ontario to Georgian Bay on Lake Huron, and from there on into the vast natural resource treasure house of the Canadian north and west.

In its aboriginal form the Passage had two main arteries — one on the west, broadly following the Humber River, and one on the east following the Rouge. Both finally came to focus on the Holland River, which flows north to Lake Simcoe (which then leads to Georgian Bay). The old secret of Newmarket is that it lies at a ford across the Holland River. What is still called Main Street in the original village runs north from this particular stretch of water. In the early 19th century the place was a last outpost of the multiracial "Indian-European" fur trade in Southern Ontario.

The modern secret of Newmarket is that, even during its early fur trade romance, a very rough and ready version of Yonge Street already came crashing through the forest — not too far west of the Main Street that follows the Holland River. It was in fact the Ontario, Simcoe & Huron Railway (another 19th century modernization of the ancient Toronto Passage) that inspired Newmarket's incorporation as a village separate from Whitchurch Township, in 1858. A century later the growing automobile traffic on a much improved north Yonge Street began to shape the rapidly growing present-day exurban town in the GTA.

Looking north on Main Street (from the Water Street ford on the river)

Seen in this context, Newmarket today is just the most northerly in a trio of rising urban centres focused vertically along Yonge Street. (The other two are Aurora and Richmond Hill). Newmarket was home to less than 25,000 people in the middle of the 1970s. By 2001 the number was more than 65,000 — well over half of whom had moved into new housing in the past two decades.

On a cool and windy day in the autumn of 2001, it makes sense to stop off at an old-style diner on Main Street in the old village, not far south of Davis Drive. When you leave the restaurant and walk a short distance north, to Main Street and Davis Drive, you are suddenly in a much more up-to-date early 21st century suburban sprawl, just north of the big-city heartland, full of automobiles and fast-food outlets and convenience stores in strip malls.

Davis Drive and Main Street, looking east

On some parallel pattern old Newmarket was concentrated to the east of Yonge Street, but today's new town is shifting west. The rising local centre of retail commerce is Upper Canada Mall, on the northwest corner of Davis Drive and Yonge Street (a kind of companion, one might guess, to Upper Canada Place in Burlington).

You cannot yet quite say that Yonge Street has become the new main street of Newmarket. The great bulk of the present-day town — including most of its industrial land — still lies to the east. Yet the Glenway Estates subdivision, stretching from Yonge all the way to Bathurst, and from Davis Drive south to Mulock Drive, does already occupy a substantial new chunk of western turf.

To both the north and south of Glenway Estates there are plans for new tract-housing subdivisions in the west end of Newmarket. Already they are sketched in on the latest commercial maps of the GTA — streets of the future just waiting for more new people who need new places to live. They will be brand new places, with new plumbing and heating systems, roofs that don't leak, and garages for the family cars. Yet you will still feel that somehow you have gone back to the land. You are a pioneer again, in the 21st century.

In fact, Yonge Street is already the main street for the Newmarket that is, so to speak, the capital of York region. The administration centre or head office for the entire region is located on the west side of Yonge, somewhat south of Davis Drive. It is a legacy of Newmarket's earlier history as the seat of the old York County.

York Region Administrative Centre, 17250 Yonge Street

Like the Living Arts Centre in Mississauga, the new public facility here has been controversial. The local historian Robert Terrence Carter has explained: "As the huge structure went up on its Yonge Street site during 1992 and 1993, so too did its cost of construction," ultimately rising to "several times the initially budgeted figure." The "end result was a spectacular building of curved surfaces and vaulted spaces." But in the last half of the 1990s it was also a spectacular example of hard-earned tax dollars wasted by government.

Standing in the wind outside the place in the autumn of 2001, with September 11 on television still too much on your mind, you might wonder again. Maybe interesting and even expensive new public buildings still help stitch peace, order, and public security into the local social fabric, or something like that. However you choose to see such things, the York Region Centre is no doubt some kind of advantage for Newmarket today.

13
AURORA

You could call the Town of Aurora a rose between two thorns. This would not be exactly correct. Neither Newmarket, due north, nor Richmond Hill, to the south on the Yonge street corridor, is a thorn at all. But Aurora is nonetheless somewhat more exclusive. It has fewer residents, and a considerably higher average income — almost as high as in neighbouring Whitchurch-Stouffville or King, or Oakville much further to the south and west.

Aurora also has its own old buildings from the local past. In the Whitchurch Township of the early 19th century a hamlet known as Machell's Corners arose around businesses operated by the Machell family, at Yonge and Wellington streets. Then, as in Newmarket, the subsequent arrival of the Ontario, Simcoe & Huron Railway east of Yonge Street brought a fresh burst of growth.

According to the legends of the present, in 1854 the name of the hamlet

Machell House, 17 Wellington Street East, built ca. 1861 for Henry Machell, son of one of the town's first merchants

at Machell's Corners was changed to Aurora "to herald the dawn of a new age." (It was both the new age of the railway and what international historians nowadays call "the world boom of the 1850s." And note that "aurora" means "dawn" in Latin.) In 1863 Aurora was incorporated as a village separate from Whitchurch Township. In 1888 the village was re-incorporated as a town.

In late October 2001 it seems unclear whether another new age of the Internet is being accompanied by yet another world boom. (Or maybe world booms just typically involve assorted world busts and tragedies too.) Aurora has in any case grown from about 14,000 people in the mid-1970s to well over 40,000 today.

The present town territory is larger than it used to be, but still takes up only a modest 47 square kilometres of land, much of which was formerly occupied by family farmers. Yet this has been more than e-nough to accommodate all the new arrivals of the past quarter century, in new subdivision housing with something of a calculated upscale tilt. There is still room for considerably more to come.

Old Medical Hall (1855) 15233 Yonge Street

Unlike Newmarket, Aurora has had Yonge Street as its main thoroughfare from the start. Its many surviving old buildings still give the place some kind of 19th century look, updated by automobile traffic and more recent in-filling and new construction.

Aurora

Many of the old buildings are serving new and updated purposes. What is sometimes said to be the town's original skyscraper — the intriguing three-storey Old Medical Hall erected in 1855 — has had a long subsequent but now ended history as a drugstore.

Just south of the Old Medical Hall, the Old Post Office on Yonge Street dates from 1915, in the middle of the First World War. As the town website explains, it still boasts "a fine Tuscan tower" that "also houses the town clock." It no longer serves as a post office. But renovated office space for dentists and related professionals (including Smile Dental and the Dentrax Dental Library) have picked up some of the slack left by the Old Medical Hall.

Further south on Yonge, and around the corner on Church Street, is the former Aurora Public School — as a plaque in front notes, "constructed in 1886" and "one of the finest remaining examples in Ontario of a public school designed in the High Victorian manner." It now serves as "the home of the Aurora Museum and other community groups."

Old Post Office
15213 Yonge Street

Today's official Town of Aurora website also stresses that "Lester B. Pearson attended this school." Pearson was the 1960s prime minister of Canada who had earlier won the Nobel Peace Prize, for his diplomatic role in resolving the Suez Crisis of 1956. Then he finally gave his country its own flag, in 1965. After his death, he was the inspiration for the present name of the Lester B. Pearson International Airport, in the northwest corner of Mississauga.

In fact, Lester "Mike" Pearson was the son of a Methodist clergyman, whose family moved every few years, as was the custom of the day. In 1901 the future prime minister started kindgergarten at the old Aurora Public School. Not much later he moved on.

In his early 1970s memoirs, Pearson nonetheless did remember his brief stay at Aurora Public School, when the sun still "never dared to set" on the old British empire, even in Southern Ontario. He also recalled how in 1901 "Miss Lois Webster, my teacher, held my hand to show me how to write, or rather trace the word 'cat!'"

Grounds of the old Aurora Public School (1886), 22 Church Street

A hundred years later the more numerous people of early 21st century Aurora, like almost everyone else in Ontario, were regularly voting for Pearson's Liberal successors in Canadian federal elections. In Ontario provincial elections, like the majority elsewhere in the outer or 905 subregion of the GTA, they were regularly voting for the somewhat belated local neo-conservative emulators of Margaret Thatcher in the UK, and Ronald Reagan in the USA.

Like all of Canada, perhaps, Aurora — always waiting for the dawn of another new age — has learned to hedge its bets. Who would even try to predict what the federal or provincial political future will bring, to say nothing of continental or international politics, or further booms and busts in the world economy? Whatever happens, according to the town website, by 2026 Aurora is planning for more than 75,000 people, and 33,000 jobs.

14
RICHMOND HILL

As you keep moving south on the north Yonge corridor, you get closer and closer to the throb of the big city. The Town of Richmond Hill now has almost twice as many people as Newmarket, and more than three times as many as Aurora. Between 1991 and 1996 it was the GTA's fastest-growing area municipality. Between 1996 and 2001 it was second only to the adjacent City of Vaughan, to the south and west.

Richmond Hill descends from the old townships of Markham and Vaughan. The modern village is said to have begun in the early 19th century, when the Miles family established an inn, a general store, and an ashery at the intersection of Yonge Street and Major Mackenzie Drive.

Today the southwest corner of Yonge

Richmond Hill Central Library, Yonge Street and Major Mackenzie Drive

and Major Mackenzie is home to the Richmond Hill Central Library. The same general area also hosts what present-day archaeologists call the Boyle-Atkinson Site — an Iroquoian village dating back to the last half of the 15th century. As the Internet explains, this is only one of several known Iroquoian village sites in the Richmond Hill area, "all found along headwater tributaries of the Don and Rouge rivers," on the old Toronto Passage from Lake Ontario to Georgian Bay.

At this latitude the Ontario, Simcoe & Huron Railway in the middle of the 19th century emulated the more westerly branches of the aboriginal Passage, with stops at Maple and King City before veering east to Aurora and Newmarket. It did not do the emerging village at Yonge and Major Mackenzie much good. In the early 20th century the radial railway that ultimately ran from Toronto to Lake Simcoe started to improve the location. Then the arrival of the automobile on Yonge Street locked in "the concept of commuting to Toronto to work."

New housing under construction in the old Rose Capital of Canada

Richmond Hill's first modern residential subdivision was registered as early as 1910. It finally led to the growth of the present-day Richvale community. The new and more mature automobile age that triumphed in the 1960s accelerated the trend. In one way or another close to 100,000 new people appeared in town during the last quarter of the 20th century. Amidst all the new puzzles of the early 21st century, the pace of growth continues. The perpetual construction of new tract housing seems a fixed part of the landscape.

In the earlier 20th century certain residents of Richmond Hill who were not commuting to jobs in downtown Toronto acquired some fame for growing roses in greenhouses — in what became "the Rose Capital of Canada." In 1935 a group at the University of Toronto, led by Dr. C.A. Chant, established an astronomical observatory with what was then the second-largest telescope in the world, on farm land in the present southeastern part of town. The facility took its name from its benefactor, David Dunlap, "a lawyer who had become rich from mining investments in Northern Ontario, and who had an amateur's interest in astronomy."

Hillcrest Mall, south entrance near Yonge Street

By the late 20th century the much more populous and rapidly growing suburb on the higher ground due north of Toronto had become especially celebrated for its shopping malls. Hillcrest Mall, on the northwest corner of Yonge and Carrville Road (or 16th Avenue east of Yonge), has "over 115 shops and services."

Along with Markham, and Scarborough in the City of Toronto, still further to the south and east, Richmond Hill today is also celebrated for several Chinese shopping malls — upscale suburban variations on old-city Chinatown themes of lesser days gone by. The largest concentration of this current development in Richmond Hill is in the east end around Leslie Street, just north of the Highway 7 corridor that forms the town's southern boundary.

The word Richmond apparently has something to do with the attractions of the place for recent Chinese immigrants, from Hong

Kong and elsewhere. The Richmond neighbourhoods in both Vancouver and San Francisco, it has been noted locally, have large Chinese populations nowadays as well.

Yonge Street at Bantry Avenue, just north of the Highway 7 corridor

But it is not just recent Chinese immigrants who distinguish Richmond Hill in the GTA today. The local Royal LePage real estate office is prepared to do business in "more than 30 different languages! Call us and we will find someone for your language." In 2001 just over 48% of the people of Richmond Hill were born outside Canada — more than twice the proportion in either Aurora or Newmarket.

This is another side of what being so close to the big-city heartland means now. This part of the GTA in particular really is a global village — a term coined in the 1960s by the Toronto resident Marshall McLuhan. The closer you get to the throbbing heart, the more you can see this and feel its fascination. And in the south end of Richmond Hill you are already inside the circle. By the time your continuing southbound journey hits the east-west Highway 7 and 407 corridor you are right up at the edge of the official big city, in the Town of Markham and the City of Vaughan.

15
VAUGHAN

Very broadly, Italians, a few thousand mostly Chinese men, and a great many East European Jews pioneered the present-day multicultural Toronto, deep downtown in the late 19th and earlier 20th centuries. Now many such old urban pioneers have also fled to the suburbs. Many Chinese have gone to Richmond Hill and Markham. Many Jews and many, many Italians have gone to the City of Vaughan — "the City Above Toronto," as the official slogan urges, lying along the current City of Toronto's northwestern edge.

Municipal election posters in the new City of Vaughan

Strictly speaking, this probably is a little too broad. The mayor's message on the Vaughan website comes in nine languages, not just two or three: English, French, Italian, Hebrew, Chinese, German, Russian, Spanish, and Japanese. The real descendants of the Jewish, Italian, and Chinese pioneers are no longer immigrants. And in 2001 residents born outside Canada accounted for 42% of the City of Vaughan's total population — not quite like in Markham, or Richmond Hill, or Mississauga, or the official City of Toronto, but still very close to the top of the list.

On the Road in the GTA

Geographically, Vaughan today divides into five unofficial communities. One place to start is Concord, just north of Toronto's near west end. It is not much more than a giant industrial park, built around a Canadian National Railways freight classification yard. To the east is Thornhill, to the west Woodbridge, to the northwest Kleinburg, and more or less due north, Maple.

In the CNR freight classification yard, Concord

Thornhill today is much more than the Toronto suburban Jewish community in the new City of Vaughan. But on Monday, November 25, 2002, at 7 PM, the Bathurst and Clark branch of the Vaughan Public Library, in Thornhill, held a "CHANUKAH CELEBRATION WITH MICKEY LEWIN ... Back by popular demand!! "

Far to the north and west of the intersection at Bathurst and Clark, Kleinburg is an old village now in a kind of exurban no man's land between the City of Vaughan and the Township of King. As the official website explains, it is a place "where an atmosphere of early Canadian traditions and architecture still prevails." It is also the home of the McMichael Canadian Art Collection, which "features works by Canada's famous landscape painters, The Group of Seven, as well as works by contemporary First Nations, and Inuit artists."

Maple, due north of the Concord industrial area, is an old crossroads hamlet (and former rural stop on the ancient Ontario, Simcoe &

Huron Railway) that has lately blossomed into a haven for suburban tract housing. For the past few decades it has been home as well to Paramount Canada's Wonderland — "Canada's premier theme park featuring eight themed areas and more than 180 attractions."

Updated style in the old village of Woodbridge, east of Kipling Avenue

Woodbridge, in the southwest quarter of the new City of Vaughan, was once a rural Ontario village. Now it is the GTA's Little Italy in the exurban countryside. On a hot mid-morning in the early summer of 2002 it is a place especially obsessed by the fate of the Italian soccer team in the World Cup. There are Italian flags everywhere — on stores, protruding from cars driven by teenage boys, and draped around teenage girls waving from balconies.

In the end, the suburbs in North America are the suburbs. Even Italian culture has trouble making them look distinctive. But the old village's downtown commercial strip on Woodbridge Avenue has acquired a few new wisps of some sunny Mediterranean style it lacked before. Some of the adjacent tract housing includes the wrought-iron railings for which Italian immigrants after the Second World War became locally famous, as they renovated the housing stock in the near west end of old inner-city Toronto.

Woodbridge is also not the only part of Vaughan where the Greater Toronto Italian community is prominent. You can see its

On the Road in the GTA

wider influence in the names of the elected city council in 2002: Michael Di Biase, Bernie Di Vona, Mario Ferri, Joyce Frustaglio, Linda Jackson, Susan Kadis, Mario G. Racco, and Gino Rosati.

Suburban parkland in the middle of Woodbridge today

Vaughan's local political leadership has developed its own strong sense as well of the wider GTA's role in the still wider global village. The city council adopted an International Partnership policy in 1992. Vaughan, Ontario, Canada, now has formal friendship agreements of one sort or another with Delia, Lanciano, and Sora, in Italy — but also with Ramla in Israel, Sanjo in Japan, Baguio City in the Philippines, and Yangzhou in the People's Republic of China.

Still, there is some final sense in which none of this is all that noticeable as you travel through the City of Vaughan today. When you pass by a stretch of suburban parkland in the middle of Woodbridge, arranged in the usual way, you might think that this could be in Italy. But it could be a lot of other places, too.

Or, you could just say that the new City of Vaughan today finally is just another part of an older Toronto that has moved to the suburbs. And as the Hollywood movie producer from Montreal, Don Carmody, told the local CBC television news in the spring of 2002: "I can make Toronto look like anything, or anywhere, and have."

16
MARKHAM

There "is life beyond Markham," Adrienne Clarkson once told a Toronto business audience, before she became the first Chinese-Canadian governor general of Canada. Times have changed a little. But some who live here might still wonder why they ever need to be anyplace else. Due east of Vaughan, sprawling along the northeastern edge of the City of Toronto, the Town of Markham continues to pursue its distinctions.

To start with, in the early 21st century Markham is the third most populous GTA area municipality beyond the City of Toronto — after Mississauga and Brampton, and just before the City of Vaughan. The current official geography, it is said on a local website, "consists of four communities: Unionville, Milliken, Thornhill, and Markham Village." Each more or less relates to earlier countryside centres, now merged into the present town. (And it is worth stressing that, just to keep everything conveniently confusing, old Thornhill today has surviving unofficial pieces on either side of Yonge Street, in both Markham and Vaughan.)

Picket fences and heritage housing in Markham village

On the Road in the GTA

The same website reports that all four communities offer "some beautiful Canadian heritage and cultural attractions," and the term Canadian here is an especially broad and inclusive term. In 2001 more than half of all Markham residents (53%) were immigrants, or people born outside Canada.

New Kennedy Square: a Chinese mall in Markham

Some also say that Markham today is "Canada's high tech capital." In fact it is Brampton, not Markham, that hosts the global headquarters of Nortel Networks (once characterized by *Business Week* magazine in the US as "Canada's most important company"). But who can tell just what this means at the moment. Markham is, in any case, home to a branch-plant facility of Nortel's US-based rival, Lucent Technologies, and a plethora of similar business operations.

Unlike Brampton as well, Markham has the academic background identified with high technology. It can boast the second-highest percentage of residents with a university degree in the entire GTA.

A final big statistic in any comparison of the two places concerns what Canadian government statisticians call "visible minorities," or non-white or non-European residents, as others might say. In Brampton the most prominent visible minority is South Asian. In Markham it is unmistakably Chinese.

Markham

As in neighbouring Richmond Hill, there are some completely Chinese shopping malls in Markham today. The architecture is Chinese (more or less). Most of the signs are in Chinese, and business is conducted in Chinese languages. Not all those involved are Cantonese-speaking people from Hong Kong, but many are. Here again some marks left by the old empire are still showing. In this case they come from a British Crown Colony in China, won in the opium wars of the earlier 19th century, and surrendered at last in 1997.

Beyond the abstractions of statistics and technology, Markham's municipal government has earned some extra distinction by sometimes taking special note of a still quite new suburban development trend. As a recent academic report puts it: "Markham, Ontario is one of the first municipalities in North America to formally adopt a planning philosophy based on new urbanism."

Untrained minds may imagine that the

Hybrid new urbanism under construction

new urbanism is just an attempt to transplant the old urbanism of the streetcar era ("when America was urban and urbane," as the historian John Lukacs has said) to the automobile-dominated suburbs. It has a not surprisingly spotty record of success to date. The showplace in Markham so far is a neighbourhood called Cornell, east of the 9th Line, between Church Street and 16th Avenue. It is based on a community plan devised by the new urbanist architectural firm of Andres Duany and Elizabeth Playter-Zyberk, in Miami, Florida.

Cornell has its critics, including those who say it does not come at all close enough to its own goals. But on his most recent visit to inspect his handiwork, in the late summer of 2001, Andres Duany declared that it remains "the clearest textbook example" of the new urbanism in North America.

The simplest truth is that in 1970 Markham had about 35,000 people. Some 30 years later the number was more than 200,000. Most of the new housing built to accommodate all the new people has been what one critic calls "distinctly suburban in look and function." Yet Cornell and other "new urbanist and 'hybrid' projects" have also gone ahead. The municipality has plans for more than a dozen such projects.

"No Trespassing" in the new community of Olde Markham Village

It seems very unlikely that automobiles will ever be replaced by streetcars in the suburbs. Some will complain that certain hybrid new urbanist developments in Markham today have signs that read: "Private Community ... NO TRESPASSING." But there are similar signs on an old-urbanist gated community in downtown Toronto called Wychwood Park — once the home of the global village guru Marshall McLuhan. The new urbanism is at least an experiment in a world that can certainly stand such things. The optimistic view has to be that in Markham it will somehow do some sort of good.

IV
Durham Region

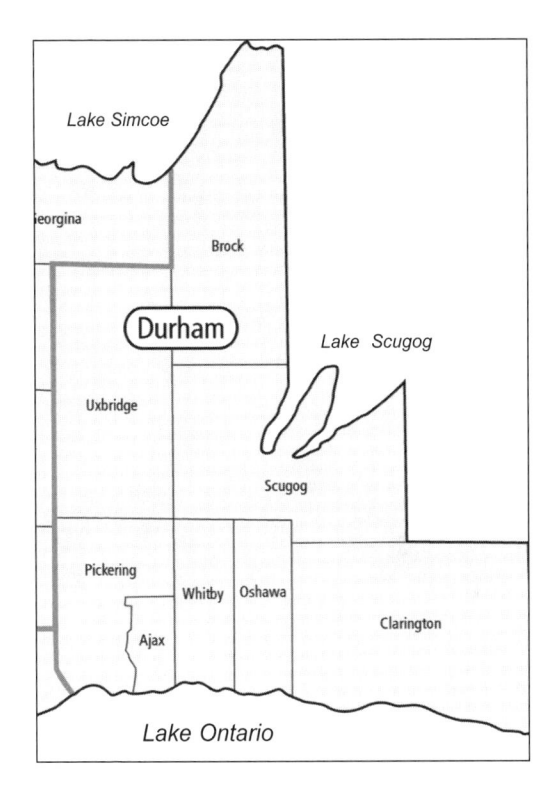

Frenchman's Bay on Lake Ontario

17
PICKERING

If you drive east on Highway 7, from Markham Road say, you will soon pass from York to Durham region — and from the Town of Markham to what is now called the City of Pickering. Here you have entered the more mysterious east end of the GTA, where things are somewhat different than in the north or the west.

About two-thirds of the City of Pickering's total land area, for one thing, is still quite relentlessly rural. This is what you are in the middle of as you drive east on Highway 7. The urban and even suburban parts of Pickering today start down on the lakeshore, due east of the City of Toronto.

To get to this demographic heartland, turn south on Brock Road when you reach the hamlet of Brougham on Highway 7. Follow Brock Road all the way south to Bayly Street. Then travel west on Bayly to Liverpool Road. Turn south again and proceed along Liverpool all the way down to Frenchman's Bay, on Lake Ontario.

Frenchman's Bay is not too far east from the mouth of the Rouge River, which now forms the most southerly eastern boundary of the City of Toronto. In the later 17th century the Iroquois village of Ganatsekwyagon stood just east of the mouth of the Rouge. Two French missionaries, François Fénelon and the Abbé d'Urfé, spent the winter of 1669–1670 in the village. The name of the bay commemorates their sojourn — said to be the first extended stay in the Toronto region by people of European descent.

A little over two and three-quarter centuries after Fénelon's and d'Urfé's winter sojourn, in the 1950s, Frenchman's Bay was an important magnet for early suburban development in the old Pickering Township. Now the more recent tract housing in the south end of the new city is clustered on either side of the Highway 401 corridor, to the north and east of the bay. It is focused around the Pickering Town Centre, Pickering Corporate Centre, Super Centre, and the Pickering Recreation Complex.

To the south and east of the bay, on the Lake Ontario waterfront, is the Pickering Nuclear Generating Station, currently operated by an organization known as Ontario Power Generation. On the Internet it is described as "the oldest atomic-power plant in Canada," and the "largest nuclear power station under one roof in the world." In the late spring of 2002 a major part of the facility has been shut down for repairs, and they are taking longer than planned.

Older suburban development to the east of Frenchman's Bay

The nuclear plant on the waterfront is part of what Pickering means today in the wider region. For the generation that has learned its nuclear plant safety from Homer Simpson in Springfield, this is hardly terrible and even quite normal. It is nonetheless one of various ways in which the east end of the GTA is different from the north or the west.

The still relentlessly rural north end of the new city is another. Part of the story here is that, in the increasingly distant past, both federal and provincial governments assembled vast tracts of land, for a second major GTA airport that is apparently still being planned.

More recently, the City of Pickering has taken to promoting the place as an efficient location for shooting certain kinds of movies. ("Just a short drive from Canada's largest city, Pickering offers an accessible country setting, ideal for film production requiring a rural flavour.") The promotion has already met with some success. Recent productions shot in Pickering include *What Girls Learn*, *John Q*, and the Canadian evening TV soap opera, "Paradise Falls."

Yet there are still not many people actually living in the north end of the new city. The demographic dynamism is in all the new tract housing in the south end — in such subdivisions as Dunbarton, Rosebank, Woodlands, Highbush, Liverpool, Fairport, Bay Ridges, and West Shore. The last three of these places are in fact still huddled around Frenchman's Bay. And Fénelon and d'Urfé's 17th century visit still points to a more romantic meaning of Pickering today.

Despite the nuclear generating station due east, over the past few decades Frenchman's Bay has also gradually been blossoming (or perhaps re-blossoming)

New development in Fairport

into something else again. It is becoming a retreat for those enthralled by the now quite ancient romance of sailboats, yachts, and other forms of nautical craft on the North American Great Lakes.

Just your naked eye will tell you that this is not the Bronte Harbour Yacht Club in Oakville. But it has its attractions. As a Canadian cruising guide explains, though "there is still occasional wreckage and construction ... many new things are happening on the east side of Frenchman's Bay," and the place is "improving all the time." As one of the organizations doing the improving summarizes the main point, Pickering today can boast "an affordable Ontario marina," which is also just a short drive from Canada's largest city.

Boat in driveway, east side of Frenchman's Bay

Along with customers who use its docking facilities for "sail boats, powerboats and fishing boats," East Shore Marina, on Frenchman's Bay, has "approximately 40 boats permanently moored year round at our docks, with their owners living aboard." Other more down-to-earth yachtspersons have settled for insulated and heated old cottages on the bay, with boats on trailers parked in their driveways. On a sunny day in the early autumn the same affordable romantic mood seems to radiate further — even out into the surrounding tract-house subdivisions and shopping malls.

In fact the wilderness sojourn of Fénelon and d'Urfé in the winter of 1669–1670, at yet another regional juncture of old canoe routes, does not seem to be widely known in the early 21st century, even on Frenchman's Bay. Yet in the new east-end GTA City of Pickering something about it still lives on, in some bizarre defining way. The past remains in the present, whether the present knows it or not.

18
AJAX

At first, the Town of Ajax, due east of the south end of the City of Pickering, along Lake Ontario, can seem a rather vague place — just more of all the tract housing and automobile traffic due west. The big question is why isn't it just part of the City of Pickering? (And to show how big a question this is, the two municipalities already share the Ajax-Pickering Transit Authority.)

The Town of Ajax from the GO station
(where the railway runs right beside Highway 401)

On closer inspection, an almost exact explanation of Ajax's unique identity can be found in the area around "Harwood Avenue/King's Crescent/Churchill Road/Roosevelt Drive," just south of the Highway 401/CN Rail/GO Transit corridor. This is the former "administrative centre for the Canadian government-sponsored Defence Industries Limited (D.I.L.) munitions plant," from the Second World War.

A still quite new plaque at the corner of Harwood and King's Crescent, erected "by Heritage Ajax Advisory Committee, September 2002," provides some further detail. The "D.I.L. complex was initiated in 1940 and eventually became the largest ammunition plant in the British Empire, employing more than 9000 workers from all parts of Canada." The "D.I.L. era was the beginning of the urbanization of this area." (Before then it was just the southeast corner of the old Pickering Township.) The "name 'Ajax' was chosen in honour of the H.M.S. Ajax, a famous World War II cruiser." In what the quite new plaque calls "The Heart of Ajax" today "most of the local street names honour the veterans of the ship."

In the early fall of 2002, just after the September 11 first anniversary, all this seems to have some fresh relevance (which helps explain the quite new plaque). But there are no defence industries in Ajax today. As a sign of just how much the world has changed since 1940, in the industrial area that straddles Bayly Street, west of Harwood, there is a Daimler-Chrysler automobile plant.

The Daimler-Chrysler facility in Ajax is not at all on the same scale as General Motors Canada in neighbouring Oshawa, or even Ford in Oakville. Something of the Second World War era, however, does seem to be living on. As you walk by on Bayly Street, you can't help noticing a group of somewhat formidable-looking women outside Daimler-Chrysler having a smoke — dressed so as to make clear that, like Rosy the Riveter, they work not in the office but on the line.

New WWII memorial in the heart of Ajax, at the old DIL Administrative Centre

Yet even in the midst of all such historical explanations, the big question about Ajax still lingers. To take a few other cases in point,

Ajax

Bayly Street in Ajax is just a continuation of Bayly Street in Pickering. If you follow Harwood south of Bayly, you pass a hospital complex called the Ajax and Pickering Health Centre. If you keep going south from here you will reach Rotary Park on Lake Ontario: to the east of this is an Ajax community called Pickering Beach.

Older housing, west of Harwood, north of 401

Most of this most southerly end of Ajax today is taken up by newer tract subdivisions. But further north, on the edge of the Highway 401 and CN Rail corridor, the older DIL area still has so-called "wartime housing" — simple wood-frame buildings quickly erected by the Canadian federal government in the early 1940s, to house munitions employees and their families.

There are some similar older residential neighbourhoods just north of the highway and rail corridor, and west of Harwood. Wartime housing stands out here too, along with a few buildings that recall the still older Ontario countryside in the former Pickering Township. A little further west again the present-day Town of Ajax is host to an earlier community called Pickering Village.

North of Kingston Road, which actually begins in the City of Toronto, there is more new tract housing, in the Westney Heights subdivisions of Riverside (by Duffins Creek), Hermitage, and

On the Road in the GTA

Applecroft. To the north of here, and to the east generally, Ajax still has some open countryside, waiting for more new subdivisions.

Based on current trends, quite a few of Ajax's future subdivision residents will be immigrants, or people born outside Canada. In 2001 the town had the ninth-highest percentage of immigrants in all 25 GTA municipalities (at 25%).

Ajax today is in particular a home to substantial numbers of what federal statisticans call Black immigrants from various regions of the globe, including the USA. There is some wider earlier history here. Before the American Civil War, Southern Ontario was a destination on the Underground Railroad, bringing fugitive slaves to at least one 19th century kind of freedom. The history of most people of African descent in Ajax today, however, starts with much more recent migrations.

St. Nedela Macedonian Orthodox Church, Bayly Street

As elsewhere in the GTA, no single cultural group of any variety finally dominates the local area. The point is brought home by the new premises of the St. Nedela Macedonian Orthodox Church on Bayly Street. Its Byzantine contours remind you that Alexander the Great was a Macedonian. Ajax himself was originally a great figure of strength in Greek mythology. Only time will tell whether this is enough to keep the Town of Ajax forever separate from the City of Pickering. Meanwhile, the big question lingers on.

19
UXBRIDGE

You could just keep going east from Ajax, along the waterfront into the Town of Whitby — which is somewhat to the City of Oshawa as the Town of Ajax is to the City of Pickering. It makes more sense, however, to explore the three very sprawling countryside municipalities in the north end of Durham region first.

At the edge of the old town of Uxbridge

To start with, there is the fabled Uxbridge Township. To get here from Ajax try Salem Road in the north end of Ajax. Then jog from there to Balsam Road in Pickering, and from there to the 7th Concession in Uxbridge Township, which turns into Main Street in the old town of Uxbridge, in the township's middle east end.

In some parts of downtown Toronto today, Uxbridge is fabled as the place you should go if you have altogether lost patience with the increasing density and disorder of the post-modern inner city. It is a corner of the GTA where the tighter values of earlier eras live on brazenly: where the way it used to be is still the way it is.

There is probably quite a lot to challenge in this local stereotype. But something about it does somehow add up. If you are in the right mood, you may feel it in the prominent First World War memorial in front of the public library, on the southeast corner of Brock and Toronto streets in the old town of Uxbridge.

A very short distance away the theme carries on in an expansive outdoor mural, painted in sepia on the side of a building. It draws more attention to the era of the First World War. Dressed-up people are gathered for a parade down a muddy Main Street. They are accompanied by a small band and a few discreet flags of the old United Empire. A banner is stretched high across the street: GOD BLESS OUR SPLENDID MEN ... SEND THEM SAFE HOME AGAIN.

Back in the early 21st century, there are signs that, even in Uxbridge, things have actually changed quite a lot. An alluring bakery on Brock Street still displays mom and apple pies in its front window. But you can see as well a flyer headed BEBOP, advertising an upcoming jazz concert in neighbouring Port Perry (in Scugog Township to the east). It will feature the tough, urbane torch singer Lynn MacDonald, drummer Norman Marshall Villeneuve, and several other players — all sometime denizens of the smoky Rex Hotel on Queen Street West, in downtown Toronto's utter depths.

At the same time, the unusually named Toronto Street in the old town of Uxbridge suggests some longstanding urbanity in the wider

WWI memorial, Uxbridge Public Library

countryside here. The place has old artistic traditions too. The Canadian painter David Milne had a studio in town during the 1940s. The Roxy theatre on Brock Street — a very sleek and cosmopolitan example of a small-town movie house — echoes some similar era.

Roxy theatre on Brock Street

A plaque near the library explains "The Founding of Uxbridge." It tells how "settlement of this area was stimulated by the arrival about 1806 of approximately twelve Quaker families from Pennsylvania." Almost 200 years later, a commercial strip close to some new tract housing at the edge of the old town is anchored by an up-to-date but rather austere store called Quaker Convenience.

From this same location, you can also start to appreciate that the old town is not all of Uxbridge Township today. Only a few hundred yards from the Quaker Convenience store you are in the middle of farmland. To the south and north there are such smaller hamlets as Goodwood, Sandford, Zephyr, and Leaskdale.

Even the farmland in Uxbridge has an air of old civility. As in Whitchurch-Stouffville, or King, or Caledon, you can buy what the real estate agents call equestrian properties in the countryside here. In a still more northerly echo of the adjacent City of Pickering's north end, the Canadian Broadcasting Corporation used "the former Robert

On the Road in the GTA

Nesbitt farm on the 6th Concession" of Uxbridge Township as a main set in its "Road to Avonlea" television series, in the earlier 1990s.

Butternut Farm, Uxbridge Township

From this point on, the plot just gets thicker. The "Road to Avonlea" series was based on Lucy Maud Montgomery's genteel novels about the adventures of the civilization on which the sun never dared to set in the backwoods of Canada. Some of them "were penned ... in her Leaskdale Manse" — in northeast Uxbridge Township.

And then, about the same time as depicted in Ms. Montgomery's books (more or less), in the real world the father of Thomas Foster was running the Leaskdale Hotel. Thomas Foster himself would go on to become "a butcher in Cabbagetown in Toronto," and then a municipal politician who finally "served as mayor of Toronto from 1925 to 1927" (and "also made a large fortune from real estate").

After a visit to the Taj Mahal in India in his old age, "Foster was inspired to build a memorial temple in his boyhood community, with a Christian adaptation." This impressive enough structure was erected in 1935–1936 at a cost of $250,000. It stands on the 7th Concession, between the old town of Uxbridge and the hamlet of Leaskdale. It is now owned by Uxbridge Township, and managed by a community group called Friends of the Foster Memorial.

20
BROCK

From Leaskdale in Uxbridge it is only a hop, step, and a jump further east into Brock Township — which boasts a number of sheer statistical distinctions in the Greater Toronto Area today. It is, for instance, the most altogether northerly GTA municipality, ultimately stretching further along the northeast shoreline of Lake Simcoe than the neighbouring Town of Georgina, in York region.

At the mouth of the Beaver River on Lake Simcoe

Sprawling on either side of Highway 12, which doubles as the northbound Trans Canada Highway in this part of Ontario, Brock also takes up a quite large stretch of countryside. But it is the least populous of all GTA municipalities — home to a mere 12,110 people in 2001. And it is the municipality with the lowest average income, lowest percentage of immigrants, and third-lowest percentage of university graduates (after Georgina, and Oshawa down south).

Sheer statistics, on the other hand, can be misleading. What you can see of the social structure in Brock has less of the ups and downs that stand out in such Georgina locations as Jackson's Point. The low average income, some would say, reflects a different exurban countryside lifestyle, more than anything that seriously qualifies as visible material anxiety. On a sunny early afternoon in August 2002 there are parts of Brock Township that look rather prosperous.

The Strand Theatre in Beaverton

The Strand Theatre in Beaverton, on the shores of Lake Simcoe, is not as stylish a place as the Roxy in Uxbridge. But it seems a comfortable enough spot, where you can watch the latest movies from Hollywood, just like anywhere else. Right beside it is a small variety store, where kids still leave their bikes haphazardly on the sidewalk in front when they go in, with no worry that someone will take them.

Beaverton is just the largest of the three main small urban centres in Brock around which the present municipal population is clustered. There is also Sunderland, on Highway 12 in the south of the township, and then Cannington, to the northeast of Sunderland. The geographical feature connecting all three places is the Beaver River.

Ambitious hikers can follow the Beaver River Wetland Trail, all the way from Sunderland to Cannington. Sunderland is perhaps only half the size of Cannington, with the Beaver River just to the east. The river runs right through Cannington, which is home to both self-employed functionaries of the old countryside capitalist gentry, and staunch partisans of the ostensibly socialist New Democratic Party.

Beaverton is where the Beaver River meets Lake Simcoe. It is about twice the size of Cannington, especially when you include its modest adjacent suburbs of Ethel Park and Cedar Beach. There is a First World War memorial remarkably like the one in the old town of Uxbridge near the Beaverton Public Library. The library also has an attractive new Peg Baillie Wing. Close by is Alexander Muir Park.

Muir was the author of the proscribed old English-Canadian anthem, "The Maple Leaf Forever." He was also "principal of Beaverton Public School, 1876–1879." His song's stark allusions to how Wolfe, the conquering British hero, bore in upon the French at Quebec City in the 18th century have become altogether outdated. As if to compensate, today's Alexander Muir Park in Beaverton hosts a soothing iron-work sculpture of seagulls in flight, by the much more progressive Toronto sculptor of the later 20th century, Gerald Gladstone.

Gerald Gladstone sculpture in Alexander Muir Park

Back in the 19th century there was also an old mill in Beaverton, on the banks of the Beaver River, just before it reaches Lake Simcoe. You still come across it if you follow Simcoe Street to the waterfront, where the street turns into another beckoning long concrete pier. The adjacent land on the river has become a public park.

On the Road in the GTA

On this sunny summer afternoon, young teenage boys are putting on a dazzling display of skate-boarding skills in the park. The fever reaches its height when two girls in jeans and T-shirts lie on top of each other, on the ground in front of a ramp. If the boys come off the ramp correctly they will soar over the girls in the air. If they don't, the girls could get hurt, seriously enough. But all the boys who attempt the feat manage it without much trouble.

Old mill on the Beaver River

A little closer to the lake from here, along Simcoe Street, there is a local historical museum in the park by the river, housed in a neatly restored pioneer log cabin. The new GTA pioneers with their vast stretches of suburban tract housing (the log cabin's ultimate, technologically up-to-date successor in North America) have yet to arrive in Brock Township in any great numbers.

Yet the Gerald Gladstone sculpture in Alexander Muir Park in Beaverton, erected as a millennium project in the year 2000, seems a straw in the wind. Places like Sunderland and Cannington and Beaverton, on the Beaver River, are still largely undiscovered treasures in the new exurbanopolis. You leave them feeling that the next big burst of growth in central Ontario will start to change all that.

21
SCUGOG

Following Highway 12 due south from Sunderland will finally take you into Scugog Township — named after the unusually shaped and somewhat artificial lake that forms its northeastern boundary. Even today the sheer sound of the aboriginal word "scugog" describes something about both the lake and the township.

Houseboat on the shores of Lake Scugog

Part of the story is that until a dam on the Scugog River flooded the area around Port Perry in the earlier 19th century, Lake Scugog was considerably smaller than it is now. According to the Internet, the "term scugog actually means valley of the shallow water."

What the sound of the word implies beyond this is probably best left to the imagination. That, some would say, is part of its charm, and the shores of Lake Scugog in the early 21st century can certainly be a charming place.

Here again, as well, there are some local distinctions. The first involves some of the same Mississauga who moved into Southern Ontario during the fur-trade beaver wars of the late 17th and early

On the Road in the GTA

18th centuries, and then much later gave their name to the present-day GTA's second-largest city. Down in the less populous east of the new exurbanopolis, however, the "Mississaugas of Scugog Island First Nation" have survived as a federally registered Canadian Indian band. Nowadays they operate "the Great Blue Heron Charitable Casino facility to help with community growth and development." (For more information you can consult their website.)

According to the township website, Scugog today also "boasts some of the finest and most scenic farmland in Southern Ontario." It has over 400 farms on "more than 68,000 acres of land." And it can claim an assortment of surviving crossroads settlements and hamlets, including such places as Greenbank, Blackstock, and Caesarea.

Yet the old village of Port Perry was present at the creation of the modern countryside in

Port Perry Town Hall, 1873 (now a local theatre)

the earlier 19th century, along with the Mississaugas of Scugog Island First Nation. It remains the anchor of its surrounding area — and the home of the municipal offices for today's Scugog Township.

For some in the old downtown of the City of Toronto, Port Perry still seems a remote and doubtful part of the GTA. Visiting the place in person, in the very late long hot summer of 2002, you can start to see that this is no longer quite true.

Scugog

Right down on the lake, behind a supermarket, there is a kind of airport for model airplane flying. As intriguing as this is, it does seem remote from the Toronto inner city. Especially on a sunny day in the late summer, on the other hand, Queen Street in downtown Port Perry can strike a mildly intoxicating small-urban pose, which already attracts substantial numbers of visitors.

Queen Street in Port Perry, late summer 2002

In the summer heat you can smell the new pine shelves that have just been installed at Willow Books on Queen Street. The owner and operator has also run bookstores on Bloor Street in the Toronto core. He has been in Port Perry for four years. From him you can discover that the Toronto singer Lynn MacDonald — whose local jazz concert was recently advertised in the bakery window in nearby Uxbridge — now lives in Port Perry too.

Back out on Queen Street you can stop in at the Piano Café for tea or juice, and a sandwich or various baked goods. Something of the genteel small urbanity that older residents have struggled to carry over from the 19th and earlier 20th centuries is quietly but firmly on display here (though no one is actually playing the piano).

One of the local historic claims to fame is that in 1845 Port Perry was the birthplace of "Dr. David Palmer, the Founder of Chiropractic medicine." As a relevant website explains, the old village "dedicated Palmer Memorial Park at a ceremony that 1500 townspeople and chiropractors witnessed in a drenching rainstorm on July 28, 1938." In 1946 "a bronze statue of Dr. Palmer was unveiled and in 1961 Dr. Palmer's grandson purchased the house on Old Simcoe Street which was believed to be Dr. Palmer's birthplace" (and which "now serves as a museum known as the Palmer House").

Gateway to planned Melody Homes subdivision

Local charms of this sort are gradually drawing new people. The population of the place has virtually doubled since the mid-1970s. In the late summer of 2002 you can walk up to the gateway of a Melody Homes subdivision — some planned but not quite yet started new tract housing, at the edge of Port Perry. It announces one of several area locations awaiting new residents.

For the moment, they are not coming in any formidable rushing stream. Between 1996 and 2001 Scugog did not grow as fast as Oakville or Pickering or even Uxbridge Township, to say nothing of Whitby or Caledon or Vaughan. But it did grow somewhat faster than it had between 1991 and 1996. Its relative percentage population increase was greater than in the City of Toronto. Progress still has a somewhat different meaning here, but it is progress all the same.

22
WHITBY

Continuing to follow Highway 12 due south, out of Scugog Township, will take you to the Town of Whitby. Here the highway turns into Baldwin Street, and then Brock Street, which runs down to the Lake Ontario waterfront, and the home base of "226 R.C.S.C.C. Whitby Sea Cadets." Once again we are back on the lakeshore that gives the entire GTA its main cutting edge.

Whitby Sea Cadets on Lake Ontario

As noted earlier, the Town of Whitby is somewhat to the City of Oshawa due east, as the Town of Ajax is to the City of Pickering due west. But some emphasis has to be placed on "somewhat." Whitby is no urbanizing late bloomer from as recently as the Second World War. Its current main magnets for new tract housing and population growth — known on the town website as Downtown Whitby and the Village of Brooklin — date back to the first half of the 19th century.

You could say that, in some primordial small-town past, Whitby was just the better side of the tracks in the raw smokestack city of Oshawa. This itself is a distinction, however, and it survives in present-day local income disparities. (In fact the main railway lines in this case link rather than separate Oshawa and Whitby. But in 1996 the average income in Whitby was some $5,000 greater than in Oshawa: less than $1,000 separated Ajax and Pickering due west.)

Saturday jazz matinee on Brock Street

Whatever else, downtown Whitby has a historic main intersection, at Brock and Dundas streets, otherwise known as Highways 12 and 2. Here in 1836 Peter Perry, the local lumber magnate and Liberal politician who also founded nearby Port Perry, "built a store where the Bank of Commerce now stands." As the town website explains, "Highway 2 was the main road along the north shore of Lake Ontario, and Highway 12 was the road leading from Lake Simcoe to Whitby Harbour, making this an important commercial centre."

The Harbour and "Port Whitby" are still in business, and they are host to a yacht club. Much further north, on Brock Street past Dundas, in the late fall of 2001 there is a well-maintained white clapboard building from the later 19th century, with a coloured banner that says: JAZZ MATINEE ... EVERY SATURDAY ... BRIAN LIVETT & SWING MACHINE.

Whitby

Further north on Brock Street you are into the newer suburban tract housing. The Town of Whitby is not officially wedded to a new urbanist local planning philosophy, in the manner of the Town of Markham. But here as in other parts of the GTA much of the new housing being erected probably does qualify for some sort of hybrid new urbanist tag. The buildings look a bit like 19th century town houses — with the overriding addition of a big attached garage.

Hybrid new urbanist housing (infilled on Stokley Crescent)

Still further north, Brock Street (aka Highway 12) turns into Baldwin Street, and then this leads to the old village of Brooklin. In the very early 21st century the same Melody Homes that has plans for the farmland at the edge of Port Perry has an established project in Brooklin. It offers four quite interesting tract-housing models — The Campbell at $239,990, The Baldwin at $257,990, The Holliday at $266,990, and The McQuay at $290,990 — along with "an ambiance evocative of nostalgic, simpler times ... an era when neighbours were friends and looked after one another."

Judging from its Internet website, Melody Homes has neither projects nor plans in Oshawa. But for a brief time in the 1960s and

On the Road in the GTA

1970s Whitby and Oshawa were united in the Canadian federal electoral constituency of Oshawa-Whitby. This was the local home base of the scholarly Ed Broadbent, who ultimately became leader of the New Democratic Party of Canada (1974–1989).

More recently, the auto workers of Oshawa and environs have discovered that they are part of a new labour aristocracy in North America. The old federal riding of Oshawa-Whitby has, after various twists and turns, finally given way to the federal riding of Whitby-Ajax. And on one of the sometimes mindlessly rationalizing

Jim Flaherty's law office in Whitby

impulses of the most recent revolution in Ontario politics, provincial ridings have been made identical to federal ridings.

In the late fall of 2001 the provincial member for Whitby-Ajax was the Hon. Jim Flaherty, minister of finance in the not so Progressive Conservative government that made the revolution at Queen's Park. In the spring of 2002 Flaherty ran for the leadership of his party, as the candidate who most wanted to continue pressing forward with the revolution's goals, and he lost.

By the spring of 2003 the future of the party seems more inscrutable than it did a year before. Whatever happens, Jim Flaherty, LLB, will be able to come home to his law office in downtown Whitby. Following the revolutionary philosophy of "fewer politicians," he does not need a job at Queen's Park for the rest of his life.

23
OSHAWA

Immediately east of Whitby, Oshawa itself could be called the great surviving smokestack city of the GTA. The present local government would probably not agree. It talks about "The City in Motion," and stresses how, in the winter depths of February 2002, it had just "picked up two provincial Marketing Awards of Excellence at this week's Economic Developers Council of Ontario (EDCO) annual conference." Yet the plain truth is that Oshawa is still best known as the home town of General Motors Canada.

Unlike Ford in Oakville, far along the lakeshore to the west, here the old smokestack industry is no Johnny-come-lately. It started back in the late 19th century, with a local firm called McLaughlin Carriage Works.

In 1907 Sam McLaughlin, son of Robert McLaughlin, who built the Carriage Works, established the McLaughlin Motor Car Company, to manufacture automobiles powered by Buick engines imported from Detroit. (Sam's brother George was also involved, but in ways that elude any short summary.) Until the Second World War, the uniquely Canadian McLaughlin-Buick was advertised in newspapers as "Canada's Standard Car." By the end of the First World War

General Motors in Oshawa today

in 1918, however, the McLaughlin Motor Car Company had become General Motors Canada, with Sam McLaughlin as its first president.

The new automobile industry went on to mark the City of Oshawa in indelible ways. The old Genosha Hotel — cutely blending the names of both General Motors and Oshawa — is still in business downtown. The main local minor hockey team is still known as the Oshawa Generals. Eric Lindros is the most celebrated recent graduate in the NHL. But the Generals are legendary. Over more than six decades, more than 130 of their trainees have finally made it into the big league — including Jim Conacher, Ted Lindsay, Alex Delvecchio, and Bobby Orr. The team sweater used to bear a GM logo (perhaps later seen as a little too crassly commercial).

The Genosha Hotel ... still in business

Bringing fresh economic diversity to the present-day city in motion has been a longstanding objective of provincial as well as local government policy. In the 1980s the Ontario government moved some of its offices from Queen's Park in downtown Toronto to downtown Oshawa, to help promote the trend. The trick has worked in at least some degree. Downtown Oshawa — some distance to the north of both Lake Ontario and GM Canada — is bubbling quietly today.

Even so, Oshawa retains certain resolute attachments to its old industrial past. On King Street downtown, just east of what is now a

Oshawa

kind of eastern outpost of the Ontario Ministry of Finance, a venerable institution known as Mike's Place is still in business as well. In a style long abandoned elsewhere, it has a cigar and magazine store up front, and a restaurant specializing in earlier 20th century North American cuisine at the back.

To the east, north, west, and even south of the old downtown, Oshawa today does have some considerable acreage of more recent suburban tract housing. But the city in motion also has a long track record of not wanting to move too fast. Oshawa was home to about 100,000 people in 1974, and just under 140,000 in 2001. (Compare this

Mike's Place on King Street

with Oakville, which had about 65,000 in 1974 and just under 145,000 in 2001.) Over the past three decades the place has grown at a steady but rather deliberately slow pace. The policy goal, it seems, is to capture the essential benefits of the latest waves of progress, without unduly disturbing the long good order of the local universe.

In some respects, Oshawa is almost as obsessed by its earlier 20th century industrial heritage as Oakville is by its heritage of carefully crafted 19th century buildings. The legacy in this case involves more rugged folkways, but it also includes the McLaughlin family itself. Sam McLaughlin lived on in his Oshawa mansion to the ripe old age of 101. To the end of his days, he was particularly proud of his status as honorary colonel of the local 11th Ontario militia regiment.

Colonel Sam made a substantial fortune in the old industrial golden age. In later years he spent some of it on worthy causes. In the 1960s the Robert McLaughlin Art Gallery (named after Sam's father) was opened in downtown Oshawa. Today it fits into a larger complex that includes the city hall, the central branch of the public library, the Canadian Automotive Museum, and "the McLaughlin Bandshell in Memorial Park (corner of John and Simcoe Streets)."

McLaughlin Bandshell in Memorial Park

From the start of August until the middle of September 2002, the McLaughlin Bandshell hosted almost two dozen "free Concerts in the Park." They included performances by groups that specialized in pop, dance, big band, jazz, rhythm and blues, and top 40. But they also included three free concerts by the Oshawa Civic Band — a more traditional musical enterprise from the oldest industrial age.

So it seems there is the old urbanism and the new urbanism, and they are somehow linked, and Oshawa today is a place where a certain rugged branch of the old urbanism is still quite alive. One of the various things it seems to be saying is that, so long as you can avoid getting laid-off, working in a modern North American automobile factory can give you quite a nice life.

24
CLARINGTON

Immediately east of Oshawa along the Lake Ontario waterfront is the Municipality of Clarington. It is the most easterly local government jurisdiction in the GTA — and the one with the newest and in some respects the most interesting name. In a short space the still quite fresh and recent story of how Clarington got its name can stand for almost the entire story of the place today.

Newcastle Garage on King Street
Old Newcastle, Municipality of Clarington

Setting aside the present City of Toronto, at least the current versions of the names of the other municipalities in the Greater Toronto Area all date from a wave of Ontario regional government reform in the late 1960s and earlier 1970s. At that point Clarington had been reorganized into something called the Town of Newcastle — by the provincial government at Queen's Park.

On the Road in the GTA

The problem with this arrangement locally was that there had already been an old village of Newcastle. It was only one of several earlier municipalities merged into the new Town of Newcastle, on the wave of reform that finally created all of the Durham region in 1973. This bred increasing confusion and dissatisfaction for almost two decades. By the early 1990s the local free and democratic people had had enough, and took matters into their own hands.

King Street in Old Bowmanville (from the back of a parking lot)
Municipality of Clarington

As a first step, the November 1991 municipal election in the Town of Newcastle included a referendum on the question: "Are you in favour of retaining the name of the town of Newcastle?" Some 59% of the electorate voted No. Then the town council, assisted by the clerk's department, organized a remarkably open, efficient, and frugal process of public consultation for choosing a new name.

The ultimate choice combined the names of the two earlier rural municipalities that had formed the lion's share of the geographic base for the merged Town of Newcastle in 1973 — Clarke and Darlington townships. The new name of "Clarington" was accepted by the town

Clarington

council in October 1992. But to acquire full effect it had to be passed into law by the Legislative Assembly of Ontario.

This took place in the spring of 1993, with the resulting new law effective as of July 1. Official records of the debate on the requisite bill in the Assembly cast further light:

Mr Gordon Mills (Durham East): ... At first blush of this bill, you'd say to yourself, "Why are we changing the name of Newcastle to Clarington?"

Mr Chris Stockwell (Etobicoke West): Yes. why are we?

Mr Mills: If the member for Etobicoke West admits that he still remembers Bud Abbott and Lou Costello, if he's old enough, and "Who's on First Base?" this is really something about what this change is about, because if I can just enlighten the members, we have the town of Newcastle, we have the village of Newcastle, we have the town of Bowmanville, and people come into the fine municipality that I'm privileged and honoured to represent and they say they're looking for Newcastle, the town of Newcastle, and people say: "No, you've got it wrong. You mean the village of Newcastle." So they go down to the village of Newcastle and they say, "I'm looking for the town of Newcastle," and they say: "No, you've got it wrong. You mean Bowmanville. That's what you're looking at." So it really goes back to Bud Abbott and Lou Costello, like "Who's on First Base?"

Along with changing from Newcastle to Clarington, the "Town" of Newcastle also wanted to be known more generically as the "Municipality" of Clarington. This implied some mild local protest against the official naming conventions of the provincial Ministry of Municipal Affairs. Though no one seems to have quite said so out loud, it raised the point that, in the already reformed GTA, it didn't make a lot of sense to keep talking about such older concepts as cities, towns, and townships, when, down on the ground, most of the new municipalities involved combined elements of all three.

What's more, in the Town of Newcastle it wasn't just the old village of Newcastle and town of Bowmanville that were causing problems. As another sympathetic member of the Ontario Legislative Assembly alluded to in the spring of 1993, there were also such places as Courtice — an earlier sleepy hamlet due east of Oshawa, that had lately been invaded by vast acres of new tract housing. The parents of the member for Durham-York, Larry O'Connor, had lived in Courtice when it was very small indeed. But "there are a lot of people living in Courtice now; it's just incredible."

*Former Massey Manufacturing buildings
Old Newcastle*

The province was at this point under the unusual and unexpected leadership of the Ontario New Democratic Party — a distant echo of E.C. Drury's unusual and unexpected Farmer-Labour government of 1919–1923. Queen's Park finally agreed that Clarington could be called just a municipality rather than a town.

As if to show displeasure with all implied critiques of provincial wisdom, however, the Minister of Municipal Affairs did not introduce the requisite legislation in the Assembly, as might be expected. That was left to the local NDP member for Durham East, Gordon Mills. In concluding his opening remarks for the occasion, on April 27, 1993, Mills urged that, whatever else, the name change would mark "a new era for the region, something to go forward with."

By this juncture, as assorted local heritage plaques attest, the new Clarington already had a long history as an incubator for enterprises and individuals that later struck it rich in the big city to the west.

Clarington

This was where Hart Massey had perfected the farm machinery business that moved to Toronto in 1879, and developed into Canada's best-known multinational corporation in the first half of the 20th century (and finally gave Toronto Massey Hall, the Fred Victor Mission, Hart House, and Massey College). It was also the birthplace — and early journalistic training ground — of Joseph E. Atkinson (1865–1948), who went on to become the presiding sly and abrasive genius of the *Toronto Daily Star*.

Offices of The Canadian Statesman
(a local newspaper in business since 1837)
King Street, Old Bowmanville

Perhaps with such thoughts about its past at the back of its mind, the new Clarington of 1993 went on to become the third fastest-growing area municipality in the entire GTA between 1991 and 1996. It slipped to eighth place — in a field of 25 competitors — between 1996 and 2001 (when you had to be very close to the City of Toronto to stay right at the top of the list). Yet visiting the municipality in the fateful fall of 2001, you feel that it still has a lot of quietly unique and distinctive energy.

It is now home to some 70,000 people, up from less than 30,000 for the Town of Newcastle in 1974. There still is some kind of new era afoot, and Clarington is still going forward. Perhaps Oakville really is the jewel of the wider region. But it may be that, all things considered, Clarington is the most interesting place in the GTA today. It may also be that the name change has helped out.

V
The City of Toronto

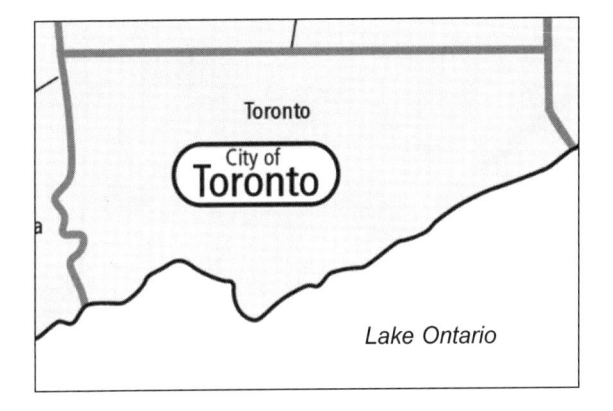

*Northwest corner King and Bay streets,
in the most inner core of downtown Toronto*

If the traffic is running smoothly on 401 (and the Don Valley Parkway), you can drive your car from Clarington to the inner city core of downtown Toronto in less than an hour. Joseph Brant's wife, Catherine, back on Burlington Beach in the War of 1812, would probably be amazed.

At the same time, it is probably also true that half a dozen seriously motivated Iroquois warriors, in a big bark canoe, could make the same journey along Lake Ontario surprisingly quickly, 350 years ago or more. And as in similar places elsewhere, nowadays you can be delayed by gridlock on the GTA road system. In the middle of December 2002 a headline in Toronto's free tabloid daily newspaper announces: GTA TRAVEL WILL GET WORSE: REPORT.

❖

There are many such problems in the naked city region. It is some kind of good sign that the people of Toronto are starting to worry. Meanwhile, in the early 21st century the first thing to notice about the big-city core of the GTA, in the official city proper, is that it is now much bigger than it used to be.

The outer 905 subregion, already rationalized in the late 1960s and earlier 1970s, was left untouched by a new wave of reforming zeal in the late 1990s. But the inner 416 subregion was a different case. In 1997 the Ontario government at Queen's Park decided to dismantle the old Municipality of Metropolitan Toronto — established in 1953 as the first working example of the "metropolitan federation plan" of local government reform in North America.

Effective January 1, 1998, the former federated cities of Toronto, North York, Scarborough, Etobicoke, York, and the Borough of East York (along with their shared wider Metropolitan Toronto bureaucracy) were all collapsed into a new amalgamated City of Toronto. The result was a "megacity," as someone first said, in a single unified space: from the Rouge River on the east to Etobicoke Creek on the west, and from Lake Ontario all the way north to Steeles Avenue.

On the Road in the GTA

The rationale was supposed to be efficiency. Yet in effect Queen's Park — now in the hands of neo-conservative revolutionaries — wound up saying that, on the one hand, it was most efficient for the somewhat more than 2.5 million people in the outer 905 subregion of the GTA to be served by 28 different municipal governments (four regions and 24 area municipalities). On the other hand, it was most efficient for the somewhat less than 2.5 million people in the inner 416 subregion to be served by a single massive local bureaucracy, and an unwieldy 45-member elected city council.

❖

On the dominant assumptions of the early 21st century, the place to start any real exploration of even the new mega Toronto is still the downtown financial district — the throbbing heart of the present-day Canadian "city with the heart of a loan shark" (as some still say in some parts of Western Canada, or Atlantic Canada, or Northern Canada, or even or especially French-speaking Quebec).

As winter sets in again, in the late days of 2002, the longer-term future of the Toronto financial district, from Yonge west to University, and Queen south to Front Street, is a subject that concerns some of those most intimately involved.

Historically, you might almost say, the Toronto financial community has been New York City's outpost in the vast and resource-rich northern North American wilderness of Canada. New York's modern presence in the Toronto region began with the Iroquois of the Mohawk Valley and what later became the Erie Canal — some of whom moved onto the north shore of Lake Ontario in the middle of the 17th century. "Toronto" itself, the latest wisdom says, is a Mohawk word, which means "trees standing in water."

Then the Iroquois were succeeded by the Mississauga, and certain westward gleanings from the Montreal-based transcontinental fur trade in Canada. The Montreal fur trade culminated with the golden age of the (in some ways) quite multiracial North West Company, in the earlier 19th century, from the Atlantic to the Arctic to the Pacific Oceans. Almost 200 years later the Canadian fur trade finally served as the object of some early jokes in the movie *Hollywood Ending*, by the well-informed Woody Allen from New York.

The City of Toronto

Deliveries on Bay Street in the financial district

It is only comparatively recently that all this earlier Canadian economic history finally came together on the northwestern shore of Lake Ontario. The more southwesterly and warmer Toronto did not supplant Montreal on the St. Lawrence River as Canada's biggest city region until the federal census of 1976.

It was not until the 1960s and 1970s that the major Canadian chartered banks began to erect soaring new office towers, more or less along Bay Street, the traditional main street of the Toronto financial district. It was 1976 as well when the Montreal-headquartered Canadian National Railways opened the CN Telecommunications Tower on the downtown Toronto waterfront (tallest structure of its sort in the world, at 553 metres or 1,815 feet).

❖

A lot has happened in the Toronto financial district since the 1960s and 1970s. Economic restructuring is an old story in Canada, ever since the fur trade gave way to the new resource economies of lumbering, wheat, and mining — and then Eaton's, Massey-Harris, and many other now vanished legends of Toronto business history.

The story's latest chapters have been driven by such controversial abstract forces as globalization, North American free trade, and continuing Canadian regionalization (in two official languages). In the winter of 2002–2003 bland Bill Davis from the GTA City of Brampton does seem to have caught the flow of the current local universe best. Like his favourite San Francisco model, Toronto today is a regional financial centre. It does business in various parts of North America and the global village (still with some special interest in the vast geography of Canada, just as San Francisco is still in California).

What all this means for the Toronto Stock Exchange — which grew out of the old Canadian resource sector — is for the moment unclear. It has just changed its official abbreviation from "TSE" to "TSX." In the winter of 2002–2003 ongoing talk of Canadian chartered bank mergers and acquisitions is in the air as well. It seems almost certain that this is going to happen soon enough. Some of the soaring downtown Toronto bank buildings of the later 20th century will be belonging to each other, or something like that.

Meanwhile, the late William McElcheran's bronze statue of two businessmen *Closing the Deal*, by the Wellington Street entrance to the present head offices of the Canadian Imperial Bank of Commerce (CIBC), somehow makes clear that, whatever happens, the city with the heart of a loan shark will be living on, and on, and on, and on.

❖

If the official City of Toronto today still starts in the old downtown financial district, some would say its most profound attraction has always been the more or less civilized and open-ended social setting it offers for ordinary life. In an older vocabulary, even the new mega-Toronto is still a city of liveable neighbourhoods.

Something of what this means is captured in another piece of public sculpture by William McElcheran — a bronze mural called *Cross-Section*, in the Dundas subway station, by the entrance to the Atrium on Bay. Here McElcheran's prototypical businessman makes another appearance, but this time in the company of many of the other characters who help make up ordinary Toronto life.

The City of Toronto

Admiring William McElcheran's businessmen
Commerce Court, Wellington Street entrance

    To appreciate the city of neighbourhoods you have to get out in the neighbourhoods themselves. There is an A-list of leafy avenues traditionally held in high esteem: the Annex, the Beaches, Cabbagetown, High Park, Lawrence Park, Moore Park, Parkdale, Rosedale, and so forth. And there are some well-known old-city ethnic shopping strips — including a Greektown and an exotic Little India in the near east end. But in the early 21st century the full range of interesting megacity neighbourhoods reaches beyond all traditional lists.

First snowfall on Humewood Drive

The stretch of the old York Township north of St. Clair Avenue, from Bathurst west to Oakwood, say (call it Humewood, after its local public elementary school), is a case in point. In its original modern urban incarnation, this was a rural area at the edge of an earlier City of Toronto, settled by in part by British working-class immigrants in the late 19th and earlier 20th centuries.

Some of these earlier immigrants came from Brixton in south London, England. The intersection of Brixton Road and Camberwell New Road, in London today, still looks a bit like an inflated version of the north intersection at Vaughan Road and St. Clair Avenue, in the City of Toronto (or of course, and more properly, vice-versa).

Nowadays as well, Brixton is famous as a centre of West Indian immigration to the United Kingdom. And as a sign of the subtle ways in which the old global empire still lingers in Toronto, even in the early 21st century, the Humewood area is a centre of West Indian immigration to Canada.

It may be that the area has less of a West Indian community in the winter of 2002–2003 than it did 10 years ago. The schoolyard shows a diverse assortment of the many different peoples from different parts of the world who live in Toronto today.

Humewood House, founded 1912

Yet both here and in the wider neighbourhood you can still see more than a few West Indian people. There are still West Indian restaurants, stores, churches, and even law offices, at various points along St. Clair and Vaughan Road. In some strangely fascinating way they are carrying on with the same generic local story started by the British working-class immigrants a century ago.

❖

Toronto neighbourhoods have long depended on some depth of public and non-profit services, to help stiffen the civility of the social fabric. In an earlier era Humewood House, on Humewood Drive just north of St. Clair, was a discreet "home for unwed mothers." Today its official Internet website more boldly declares:

Humewood House is a Young Parent Resource Center, founded in 1912. It is a non-profit, charitable organization governed by a volunteer Board of Directors and staffed by professionals and volunteers ... For hundreds of

On the Road in the GTA

young women, the walk up Humewood Drive has been the first step on the road to a happier and healthier future.

South of Humewood House, on the northeast corner of St. Clair and Humewood Drive, is the World Class Bakery and Restaurant, where you can stop for a coffee and a piece of pastry, in almost upscale inner city surroundings. Above the restaurant, on the second floor of the building, are the law offices of Charles Roach.

Several decades ago Charles Roach came to Canada from the West Indies. He studied law in Saskatchewan, and then moved to Toronto, where he developed into something of a controversial public figure. But even his critics acknowledge that he has fine manners, in the style most admired by the local civic culture.

Charles Roach is an advocate of a new Canadian republic, which would end the very last symbolic ties to the British monarchy in Canada. In May 2002, on Court Street just east of the downtown financial district, he presided over memorial services for the historical Canadian republicans Samuel Lount and Peter Matthews — hung by their necks until dead, in the same location, for their roles in the Upper Canadian Rebellion of 1837.

Nowadays, again, it is new people who are doing the remembering, but the old local stories are living on. They are rather generic — just variations on larger themes elsewhere. The Rebellion of 1837 in Toronto was nothing at all like the French Revolution. Yet it also seems true that the human processes involved do not finally depend on any crude notions of blood and biology. Every new generation of immigrants finds its own points of reference in the diversity of the modern urban story. Charles Roach was surrounded by Canadian maple leaf flags at his memorial service for Lount and Matthews.

❖

People involved in local politics will tell you that the new megacity is still haunted by vestiges of the old metropolitan federation. In its later decades, as one case in point, Metro Toronto took some pains to promote the growth of new suburban downtowns, in such places as the former cities of Scarborough and North York. (Just west of Metro, Mississauga latched onto a similar theme.)

Scarborough Town Centre station on the LRT

Part of the idea was that these new downtowns would be linked to the old downtown in the original 19th century City of Toronto by rapid public transit. To link what was called the Scarborough Town Centre up in this way, a light rapid transit line (LRT) was constructed, from the most easterly subway station at Kennedy to the Town Centre between Brimley and McCowan roads, just south of the 401.

The considered opinion among most of those professionally involved in all this now appears to be that the experiment did not work. Scarborough Town Centre is open to the same old urbanist critique as the Mississauga City Centre. It is just a suburban shopping mall, surrounded by a few new public and private sector office buildings, and too much open space. The LRT is a light that failed.

Yet riding to the Town Centre on the LRT in the early fall of 2002 suggests a few less harsh impressions. Whatever else, the trains are crowded. People are travelling to jobs at Scarborough Town Centre. When you reach the shopping mall in the still early morning, there is a long line in front of the Tim Hortons coffee stall in the food court.

Scarborough is the most easterly part of the City of Toronto today. Not all that long ago it was a rural township. Then it suburbanized very rapidly after the Second World War, with all the sometimes inhuman architecture of that era (at its very worst, even in the free world, a kind of Stalinist chic). Among young people relaxing on street corners, elsewhere in the big city, Scarborough became Cigarboro and even Scarberia: perhaps not really a place that deserved a new downtown, or an LRT.

Yet fine plants can grow in many kinds of soil. Scarborough's most celebrated native son today is the Hollywood comedian Mike Myers. He currently lives in California. But the far east end of present-day Toronto is where he first learned about Wayne's world and the international man of mystery, Austin Powers. If you keep your eyes very wide open in the Scarborough Town Centre shopping mall, you can still see the originals of vaguely similar characters.

❖

In 2001 immigrants born outside Canada accounted for 55% of the former City of Scarborough's resident population. (It also says something interesting that federal statisticians are still collecting data for the now officially "dissolved" old municipalities of Metro Toronto.)

The 55% immigrant number for 2001 includes Mike Myers's mother — originally an immigrant from Liverpool in the United Kingdom. This follows an old pattern. In the 1860s, just before the founding of the present Canadian confederation, the majority of people in the City of Toronto had been born in the United Kingdom.

In the early 21st century Mike Myers's mother is a much more unusual case. Most recent immigrants to all parts of Toronto have not been born in the United Kingdom, or even in Western or Eastern Europe. They have come from a vast assortment of places around the world. On the Scarborough LRT you are in the company of many different colours and races of people. This may not exactly be what Marshall McLuhan was getting at when he talked about the global village in Toronto during the 1960s. But it takes no imagination to see that the place has become a global village of some sort today.

It makes some related sense that in October 2002 what used to be the Scarborough city hall in the Town Centre is the site of an "Exhibition of Islamic Art and Science Dedicated to Holy Qur'an, Hosted by the Muslim Community."

Scarborough Civic Centre, October 2002

The exhibition occupies various interior public spaces on the ground-level floor of what is still known as the Scarborough Civic Centre. Its most obvious purpose is to show that mainstream Islam today is a kinder and gentler world religion. And it probably does succeed at this well enough.

Yet to many non-Muslims the exhibition must also suggest something else. Even the progressive Islam now taught at some Toronto area private schools is indeed quite different from the rather aggressively Western and North American secular and commercial culture, that has come to dominate ordinary life in Toronto (and is, in some people's estimation, not really a culture at all). It remains quite unclear, and interesting, just what impact all the diversity in the megacity today is going to have on the Toronto future.

There are a few other signs of the times in the public spaces on the ground floor of the Scarborough Civic Centre. A map of the new megacity shows how the not-all-that-old suburban downtowns, and their associated concentrations of local government infrastructure, are still helping to shape the new unified City of Toronto.

For certain administrative purposes even the amalgamated city is divided into East, North, South, and West regions. It doesn't take much of a local political memory to see these regions as the successors of the old cities of Scarborough, North York, Toronto, and Etobicoke. Even the smaller York and East York have survived to some degree in the six local community councils that have been set up (and then strengthened), to advise the larger city-wide council on certain local policy issues.

The Scarborough Civic Centre, once the headquarters of the City of Scarborough, is now playing some similar role for both the new City of Toronto's East region and the new Scarborough Community Council. And here no doubt is one of the reasons, as well, why federal statisticians are still collecting data on the now officially dissolved area municipalities of the old Metro Toronto.

❖

If you travel west on the Bloor-Danforth subway that the LRT connects with, you will finally arrive in the great bastion of what is now called the West region of the new City of Toronto, in the old City of Etobicoke (pronounced "E-toe-bih-coe").

Immigrants born outside Canada accounted for a mere 46% of Etobicoke's population in 2001 — actually a slightly lower percentage than in the City of Mississauga due west again, just outside the old Metro Toronto. (It is also intriguing to note that both Etobicoke and Mississauga had somewhat higher percentages than the 19th and earlier 20th century City of Toronto — deepest inner-city heartland of the oldest urbanism in the new metropolis, where immigrants accounted for only 41% of the local population in 2001.)

Like Scarborough, the old City of Etobicoke and present West region of the City of Toronto runs all the way from Lake Ontario north to Steeles Avenue. There is room enough in the space involved for some quite vast assortments of various human diversities — biological, cultural, economic, gastronomic, physiological, political, religious, social, and on and on.

The present-day Lake Ontario shoreline of the new City of Toronto's far west end is also the home of some still finer-grain municipal diversity from an earlier era. The original Metropolitan Toronto of 1953 had included the old city and 12 adjacent suburban municipalities. Then in 1967 a provincial government review of the metropolitan federal experiment amalgamated the 12 suburban municipalities into a more compact collection of five boroughs (four of which went on to call themselves cities). At this point the west-end waterfront Town of Mimico was absorbed by Etobicoke.

Old Mimico train station, north of the waterfront

Something of the old Mimico municipality is nonetheless still in the air in the autumn of 2002. On the east-west lakeshore railway line there is even an abandoned Mimico train station — in between the GO station and a newer VIA Rail complex. It is a small wood-frame structure in bad repair, with the windows boarded up. Someone has scrawled GHOST TOWN on the west end of the building. But you can still get inside. It apparently remains a functional place for some bold young people who live in the Mimico neighbourhood.

❖

In its heyday the main north-south artery of the Town of Mimico (itself established only in 1911) was called Church Street. It is now just the most southerly part of the Royal York Road that goes far into the northern reaches of the old City of Etobicoke.

Call it what you like, it still serves as a kind of main street for a more or less coherent neighbourhood — defined by a series of intersecting east-west side streets, from several blocks north of the railway tracks down south to Lakeshore Boulevard. Then there are the rather rugged waterfront beaches. (And the name Mimico has something to do with the now extinct passenger pigeons who once dominated the local waterfront.)

Polish Consulate on Lakeshore Boulevard

If you knew this neighbourhood before 1967 (and after 1911), when it was still the official Town of Mimico, you can find familiar landmarks in the autumn of 2002. There are vestiges of the old municipal offices on what is now called Royal York Road. Almost all the houses in Mimico today, on streets like MacDonald, Hillside, Albani, and Eastbourne, were there half a century ago.

The local public library is in the same geographic location on Stanley Avenue. But in this case what is now called the Mimico

The City of Toronto

Centennial Library is housed in newer quarters, erected in 1967 to commemorate the 100th birthday of the Canadian confederation. Now it is just one of 99 local branches in the vast and still quite good public library system of the amalgamated City of Toronto.

The books inside the library point to more recent changes in the local social fabric. Some are in English, but many are in Polish and Russian. The theme carries on in assorted storefronts down along Lakeshore Boulevard West. You can rent videos in Polish or Russian in Mimico today, buy Polish and Russian food, and plan trips at Polish and Russian travel agents. The Polish Consulate in Toronto is now housed on an old Lakeshore Boulevard urban estate.

❖

The West region (or old Etobicoke) takes up one side of today's Toronto megacity, and the East region (or old Scarborough) takes up the other side. In between are the South and North regions, sprawling along the north-south Yonge Street corridor, still the main street of the megacity at large.

The South region is the old City of Toronto, with a public-transit-friendly streetscape and allied human geography inherited from the oldest urbanism of the 19th century. The North region is the old City of North York — the later 20th century suburban extension of the Toronto that has been so much shaped by Yonge Street: modern heir of the aboriginal canoe-and-portage Passage, to the resource-rich wilderness of the Canadian north and west.

North of Sheppard on Yonge Street is what probably comes closest to the jewel of the late 20th century suburban downtown strategy in Metro Toronto — the North York City Centre. This new northern urban core is right on the Yonge subway line: very directly and conveniently linked to the older southern downtown financial district around the King, Union, and St. Andrew's stations.

The outdoor centrepiece of the place is Mel Lastman Square. It is named after the long-serving remarkable mayor of the City of North York, who finally became, by a kind of engineered destiny it sometimes seemed, the first mayor of the new amalgamated City of Toronto. (And then Mel Lastman won a second election by a landslide, to give the destiny more weight and heft.)

On the Road in the GTA

Outdoor theatre at North York Centre

❖

By the winter of 2002–2003 "Megacity Mel" has become a wounded political animal: hounded by scandal and thwarted by the unwieldy new political structure of the unified city. By mid-January 2003 he has announced that he won't be running for office again. Yet the local future will probably look on him well enough. He can boast more serious accomplishments than the Thomas Foster who was briefly mayor of Toronto in the 1920s — and then erected a $250,000 memorial inspired by the Taj Mahal, in the GTA township of Uxbridge.

Meanwhile, Mel Lastman Square, in old North York, is a frank imitation of the earlier Nathan Phillips Square, in front of the downtown Toronto City Hall erected in the 1960s. Both places are graced by enclosed ponds of water that seem cool in the summer, and then convert nicely into skating rinks for the winter. Both places are named after local politicians from the now historic Toronto Jewish community, that did so much in the 20th century (along with the Italians and the Chinese and on and on) to pioneer the multicultural megalopolis of the 21st century.

The City of Toronto

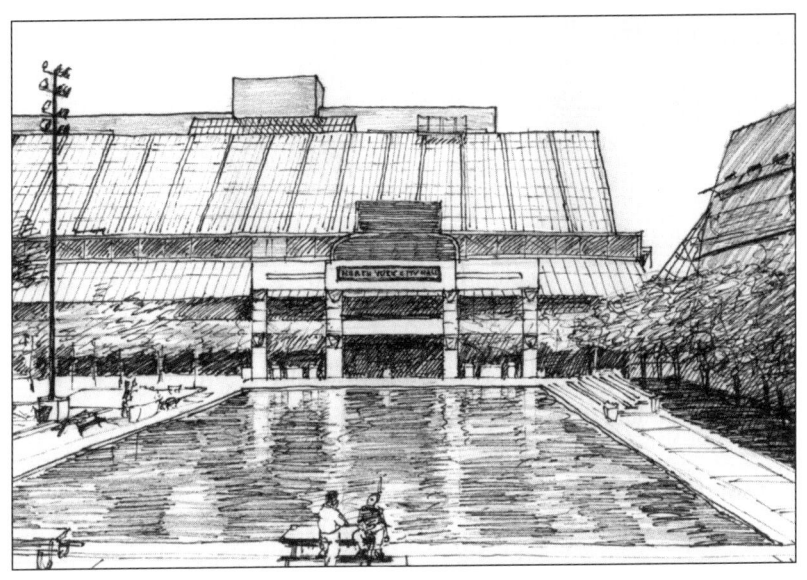

Mel Lastman Square

As it happens, the new multicultural city that *The Jews of Toronto* helped pioneer — to borrow the title of Stephen Speisman's study of their earlier history — has now attracted a growing Muslim community. In 2001 immigrants born outside Canada generally accounted for 56% of all residents in Mel Lastman's old City of North York: the greatest percentage of this sort in all of the GTA.

In the winter of 2002–2003 there is friction between some Toronto Jews and Muslims over events far away in the Middle East. Yet arcane echoes of political conflict in faraway places already have a history on the northwestern shore of Lake Ontario. An only superficially polite and restrained hostility between northern Irish Protestants and southern Irish Catholics helped energize and inspire the old City of Toronto, in the 19th and earlier 20th centuries.

It is true that a local Orange Order once had some appalling sway. But in the 1950s it was Nathan Phillips, "the mayor of all the people," who finally put what there was of an old Anglo Protestant ascendancy in Toronto municipal politics forever to rest. Almost half a century later, it was City Councillor Bas Balkissoon from Scarborough (an ethnic South Asian born in Trinidad), who took a lead in uncovering the perhaps rather vast municipal scandal over contracted-out computer services, that played a part in Mayor Lastman's decision not to run for office again, early in 2003 (and even before some remarkable TV appearances by Megacity Mel in the USA).

❖

In the winter of 2002–2003 all the diverse people in the naked city region equally have big enough problems of their own to worry about — right at home in the GTA. The bad news is always easy to come by. But the good news is that there are still reasons to keep hope alive. In a much-abused epithet that dates from the late 19th century, the city with the heart of a loan shark is also "Toronto the Good."

To start with, the movie *Chicago*, which won the Academy Award for best picture, in Hollywood in the late winter of 2003, was in fact made in Toronto, with local talent in supporting and production roles. The city's increasingly experienced cultural industry infrastructure still has trouble making good movies about its own human geography, but it has at least made it possible to start to think about such things realistically. However you look at it, there is a lot of diverse human potential in Toronto today. Another recent movie made in the city is *Bollywood Hollywood*, by the Canadian East Indian director Deepa Mehta. And it is actually set in Toronto.

Bland Bill Davis from Brampton was right a generation ago, when he stressed that Toronto will never be a place like New York (or London). San Francisco is a more realistic bench mark for the local future. But the ongoing work of building civilization in the 21st century, it seems quite reasonable to guess, will be some kind of authentically global enterprise — in which many different places participate. Like increasing numbers of cities around the world, Toronto can play some part in all this, if that is what it wants.

It already has more people and organizations known beyond its borders than it used to. It continues to attract some attention elsewhere. According to a book that just came out in 2002 (*The Rise of the Creative Class*, by Richard Florida at Carnegie Mellon University in Pittsburgh): "Cities like Seattle, Austin, Toronto and Dublin ... are striving to become broadly creative communities, not just centers of technological innovation and high-tech industry." Toronto also remains a place that stresses public civility and the importance of doing ordinary things well — the infinite attractions of ordinary life in a well-managed democracy.

By the somewhat strange local spring of 2003 several impressive heavyweight candidates have arisen to succeed Mel Lastman as new megacity mayor, in municipal elections scheduled for the fall of the year. Assorted local media outlets are making some effort to promote fresh public debate about the city's future.

In the midst of all the quietly rising new talk — still rather faintly, as the last ice and snow melts from the streets for yet another season — you can hear the bare beginnings of a particular piece of rising political wisdom. The city's future nowadays is in all of the wider city region, and not just in the city itself.

So some candidates for mayor of the City of Toronto are concerned, as they should be, about public transit in all of the GTA. Others worry about such things as the Lester B. Pearson International Airport or the Oak Ridges Moraine — both of which lie beyond even the megacity's still narrow boundaries.

Right now just what this might eventually mean, managerially and democratically, is not easy to say — except that it ought not to mean yet another new sprawling and unwieldy municipal bureaucracy. What is clear is that, more and more, "Toronto" generally means all of the Greater Toronto Area. At some point soon enough this meaning will start coming to life in fresh ways. In one respect or another, everyone in the new exurbanopolis is on the road to the GTA. The eventual destination may not prove to all tastes, but it is hard to see how it can avoid being quite interesting.

Old Newcastle
Municipality of Clarington, Durham region

Note on Sources and Modes of Travel

We visited in person at least some points in each of the 25 GTA municipalities (or 29 if you also count the four upper-tier regional municipalities in the 905 subregion). The visits took place over a two-year period, in the midst of other preoccupations.

For the most part these systematic travels were on the rails and on the road in buses, via the GO Transit system. You can visit places in all of the GTA today via GO Transit connections from Toronto Union Station, on Front Street at the south end of the downtown financial district. The GO Transit website (http://www.gotransit.com/) provides a vast array of detail. Recorded information can also be accessed by telephone. Printed schedules are available at the GO facility in Union Station.

Photographs taken during our systematic GTA travelling on GO Transit, and line drawings prepared from the photographs, became the underlying structural elements in the generation of a text for each municipality. In most cases each municipality was allocated the same amount of space, despite sometimes dramatic differences in population size. Though unrealistic in some respects, this reflects our tourists' bias. A tourist does not necessarily value one place over another because it is home to more people. Less populous places may even be more interesting to visit.

In an effort to convey some slightly more comprehensive sense of a place, beyond the points on the ground we visited in person, the text also draws on data from the Statistics Canada censuses of 1996 and 2001. Data on populations and immigration have been taken from the 2001 census. Data on incomes and education for 2001 were still not available at the time of writing, and are drawn from the 1996 census. All the information involved (and much more) can be accessed in the Community Profiles section of the Statistics Canada website (http://www.statcan.ca/).

The text draws as well on an assortment of Internet websites dealing with the GTA municipalities — starting with the official websites maintained by each of the local governments. The simplest way of accessing this material is to just enter the name of a particular municipality in your favourite search engine. We have taken *Toronto & Area 2002*, published by Peter Heller Ltd. and distributed by MapArt Publishing Corp. in Oshawa, as the ultimately definitive source for mapped information. For the general maps of the present-day GTA municipalities used in the book itself, we are indebted to Tony Romano at the Greater Toronto Marketing Alliance.

For much valued expertise in preparing both pictures and text for publication we are indebted to Jeanne MacDonald, Nadine Stoikoff, and Marie Auffrey. We are similarly indebted to Tibor Choleva and Melissa McClellan

Note on Sources and Modes of Travel

for the cover design. Larry Olsen, David Montgomery, Peter Carruthers, and Louise and Russell Reynolds provided some much appreciated technical advice on local geography and related matters. Finally, the text draws directly at various points on a number of published books and periodicals:

Anderson, Perry. "Confronting defeat ... Eric Hobsbawm's account of the making of the contemporary world." *London Review of Books*, 17 October 2002, 10–17.

Carter, Robert Terence. *Newmarket — The Heart of York Region: An Illustrated History*. Toronto: Dundurn Press, 1994.

Craig, Gerald M. *Upper Canada: The Formative Years 1784—1841*. Toronto: McClelland and Stewart, 1963.

Dale, Stephen. *Lost in the Suburbs: A Political Travelogue*. Toronto: Stoddart Publishing, 1999.

Dieterman, Frank A. (ed.). *Mississauga: The First 10,000 Years*. Toronto: eastendbooks, 2002.

Drury, E.C. *Farmer Premier*. Toronto: McClelland and Stewart, 1966.

Florida, Richard. *The Rise of the Creative Class*. New York: Basic Books, 2002.

Gagan, David. *Hopeful Travellers*. Toronto: University of Toronto Press, 1981.

Jacobs, Jane. *Cities and the Wealth of Nations: Principles of Economic Life*. New York: Random House, 1984.

Luther, Elizabeth. *Pioneering Spirit: Ontario Places of Worship, Then and Now*. Toronto: eastendbooks, 2000.

Peacock, David and Suzanne Peacock. *Old Oakville: A character study of the town's early buildings and of the men who built them*. Toronto: Hounslow Press, 1979.

Pearson, Lester. *Mike: The Memoirs of the Right Honourable Lester B. Pearson, Volume I, 1897–1948*. Toronto: University of Toronto Press, 1972.

Robinson, Percy. *Toronto during the French Regime 1615–1793*. Toronto: University of Toronto Press, 1933, 1965.

Speisman, Steven. *The Jews of Toronto: A History to 1937*. Toronto: McClelland and Stewart, 1979.

Spelt, Jacob. *Urban Development in South-Central Ontario*. Toronto: McClelland and Stewart, 1955, 1972.

Steckley, John. "Toronto: What Does It Mean?" Ontario Archaeological Society, *Arch Notes*, May/June 1992, 23–32.

Turcotte, Dorothy. *Remember the Brant Inn*. Erin, Ont.: The Boston Mills Press, 1990.

Index

Abbé d'Urfé, 83, 85–86
Acton, 18–19, 22
Ajax, 4, 81, 87–91, 103–104
Albion, 39
Alton, 39
Annex, 123
Applecroft, 90
Archaeology, 23, 69
Atkinson, Joseph E., 115
Aurora, 4, 43, 59, 62, 65–69, 72
Austin, Texas, 136
Automobile industry, 25, 88, 106–110

Baldwin, 55
Baldwin Street, 103, 105
Balkissoon, Bas, 135
Balsam Road, 91
Bantry Avenue, 72
Barrie, 5
Bathurst Street, 63, 74, 124
Bay Ridges, 85
Bay Street, 5, 118
Bayly Street, 83, 88–89
Beaches, 123
Beaver River, 96–98
Beaverton, 96–98
Beegalo Beach, 53
Belhaven, 55
Bethesda, 59
Black River, 58
Blackstock, 100
Bloor-Danforth subway, 127, 130
Bolton, 39, 41
Boston Mills, 39, 41
Bowmanville, 112–113, 115
Bramalea, 38
Brampton, 4, 27, 29, 35–42, 77–78, 136
Brant family, 10, 12, 14, 119
Brant Inn, 12
Brant Museum, 12, 14
British empire, 7, 17, 35, 68, 88, 92, 124
Brixton, 124
Broadbent, Ed, 106
Brock Street, 92–93, 103–105
Brock Road, 83
Brock Township, 4, 81, 95–98
Bronte Harbour Yacht Club, 26, 85
Bronte Road, 25–26
Brooklin, 103, 105

Brougham, 83
Burlington, 4, 9–14, 17, 23
Burlington Beach, 11, 39, 119
Burnhamthorpe Road, 31

Cabbagetown, 94, 123
Caesarea, 100
Caledon, 4, 19, 27, 29, 39–42, 45, 47, 93, 102
California, 6–7, 30, 122, 128
Canada's Wonderland, 75
Canadian Statesman, 115
Cannington, 96–98
Carmody, Don, 76
Carrville Road, 71
Carter, Robert Terrence, 64
Cedar Beach, 97
Cedar Mills, 39
Cedar Valley, 59
Cedarbrae, 55
Chant, Dr. C.A., 71
Charleston Sideroad, 39, 42
Children of Peace, 49–52
Chinese community, 34, 71, 73, 76, 79, 134
Chinese Malls, 71, 78–79
Chisholm, William, 23–24, 26
Churchill, 59
Churchill Road, 87
Clarington, 4, 81, 111–116, 119
Clark Avenue, 74
Clarkson, 32
Clarkson, Adrienne, 77
CN Tower, 14, 121
Concord, 74
Cook's Bay, 53
Cooksville, 32
Cornell, 79–80
Country Heritage Park, 15
Court Street, 126
Courtice, 113–114
Credit River, 20–21, 34
Crossroads Christian Television, 17

Dale, Stephen, 6
Davies, Robertson, 41
Davis Drive, 62-64
Davis, William (Bill) Grenville, 6–7, 35, 38, 42, 122, 136
Defence Industries Limited, 87–89
Di Biase, Michael, 76

Index

Dixie Road, 36–38
Don River, 70
Don Valley Parkway, 119
Drury, E.C., 18, 114
Duany, Andres, 79–80
Dufferin Street, 49
Duffins Creek, 58, 89
Dunbarton, 85
Dundas Street, 104
Dunlap, David, 71

East Gwillimbury, 4, 43, 49–53
East Shore Marina, 86
East York, 119, 130
Eaton Centre, 18
Eaton's, 46, 122
Egypt, Ontario, 55
Elmhurst Beach, 53
Ethel Park, 97
Etobicoke, 119, 130–133

Fairport, 85
Fénelon, François, 83, 85–86
Financial district, 120–122
Flaherty, Jim, 106
Florida, Richard, 136
Ford Drive, 23, 25
Foster, Thomas, 94, 134
Frenchman's Bay, 82–86
Front Street, 120

Gagan, David, 29
Gage Park, 36–38
Ganatsekwyagon, 83
Georgetown, Ontario, 19–22
Georgian Bay, 61, 70
Georgina, 4, 43, 53–57, 95
Gladstone, Gerald, 97–98
Glen Abbey, 25
Glenway Estates, 63
Globe and Mail, 36
GO Transit, 7–8, 13, 24, 26, 44–45, 58, 87, 131, 139
Goodwood, 93
Graham Sideroad, 49
Grand River Valley, 14
Greater Toronto Airports Authority, 32
Greek community, 32, 48, 123
Greenbank, 100

Halton County Court House, 16
Halton County Radial Railway Museum, 17–18
Halton Hills, 4, 9, 19–23, 39–40
Hamilton, 5, 11–13
Hampton, Lionel, 12
Harwood Avenue, 87, 89
Hermitage, 89
High Park, 123
Highbush, 85
Highway 2, 104
Highway 7, 71–72, 83
Highway 12, 95–96, 103–105
Highway 48, 57
Highway 401, 15, 19, 21, 30, 83, 87, 89, 119
Highway 403, 30
Highway 407, 72
Hillcrest Mall, 71
Holland Landing, 51–52
Holland River, 51, 58, 61–62
Hong Kong, 5, 71–72, 79
Humber River, 46, 61
Humewood neighbourhood, 124–126
Hurontario Street, 40

Immigrant population, 20, 25, 32, 36, 48, 72–73, 75, 78, 90, 95, 124, 128, 130, 135
Income, 40–41, 57, 95, 104
Inglewood, 39
Iroquoian peoples, 14, 69–70, 83, 120
Italian community, 32, 73–76, 134

Jackson's Point, 54–56, 95
Jacobs, Jane, 6
Jewison, Norman, 40
Jewish community, 73–74, 134–135
Joshua's Creek, 24

Keele Street, 45–46, 48
Kerouac, Jack, 7
Keswick, 53
King Township, 4, 43–49, 57–58, 65, 74, 93
King's Crescent, 87
Kingston Road, 89
Kipling Avenue, 75
Kitchener-Waterloo, 5
Kleinburg, 74

Lake Simcoe Arms, 56
Lakeshore Boulevard, 132
Lakeshore Road, 12, 23, 25, 29
Lastman, Mel, 133–137
Lawrence Park, 123
Leaskdale, 93–94

Index

Lennox, Edward, 22
Leslie Street, 49–51, 53, 71
Lester B. Pearson International Airport, 32, 67, 137
Light Rapid Transit in Scarborough, 127–128, 130
Lincolnville, 59
Lindros, Eric, 108
Liverpool, 85
Liverpool Road, 83
Living Arts Centre, 30–32, 64
Lloydtown, 46
Lock, Teffi, 54
London, England, 7, 124, 136
Lount, Samuel, 126
Lukacs, John, 79

MacDonald, Lynn, 92, 101
MacDonald Street, 132
Machell family, 65
Mackenzie, William Lyon, 50
Main Street, 20–22, 36, 59–62, 91–92
Major Mackenzie Drive, 69–70
Malton, 32
Maple, 70, 74
Markham, 4, 36–37, 43, 71–73, 77–80, 82, 105
Massey family, 114–115
Massey-Harris, 122
Matthews, Peter, 126
McCallion, Hazel, 30, 34
McElcheran, William, 122–123
McLaughlin family, 107–110
McLuhan, Marshall, 72, 80, 128
McMichael Canadian Art Collection, 74
Mehta, Deepa, 136
Melody Homes, 102, 105
Metropolitan Toronto, 119, 126, 130–131, 133
Miami Beach, 53
Miles family, 69
Mill Street, 21
Milliken, 77
Mills, Gordon, 113–114
Milne, David, 93
Milton, 4, 9, 15–20, 39–40
Mimico neighbourhood, 131–133
Mingus, Charlie, 12
Mississauga, 4, 23, 27–36, 40–41, 64, 67, 73, 126–127, 130
Mississauga people, 23–24, 30, 99–100, 120
Mistywood Park, 41

Model airplane flying, 22, 101
Mono Road, 39
Montgomery, Lucy Maud, 94
Montgomery, Wes, 12
Montreal, 41, 76, 120–121
Moore Park, 123
Motion picture industry, 84–85, 136
Moulds, William, 24–25
Mount Albert, 51–52
Mount Pleasant, 55
Muir, Alexander, 97–98
Mullett Creek, 32
Mulock, Alfred, 54
Mulock Drive, 63
Muskoka, 34
Muslim community, 128–129, 135
Myers, Mike, 128

New Kennedy Square, 78
New urbanism, 79–80, 105
New York City, 6–7, 120, 136
Newcastle, 111–114
Newmarket, 4, 43, 59, 61–66, 69, 72
Niagara Escarpment, 19
Niagara Falls, 11
Nobleton, 46
North York, 119, 126, 130, 133–136

Oak Ridges Moraine, 47, 58, 137
Oakville, 4–5, 9, 16, 23–29, 37, 65, 85, 88, 102, 107, 109, 116
Oakwood Avenue, 124
Olde Hide House, 20, 22
Ontario, Simcoe & Huron Railway, 45, 62, 65, 70, 74–75
Ontario Street South, 18
Orange Order, 135
Oshawa, 4, 81, 88, 91, 95, 103–111, 113

Palgrave, 39
Palmer, Dr. David, 101–102
Parkdale, 123
Peacock, David and Suzanne, 24–25
Pearson, Lester B., 32, 67–68, 137
Pefferlaw, 55
Phillips, Nathan, 134–135
Pickering, 4, 81–87, 91, 102–104
Playter-Zyberk, Elizabeth, 79
Pleasantville, 59
Polish community, 32, 132–133
Port Credit, 32
Port Perry, 92, 99–102, 104–105

Index

Pottageville, 46
Preston Lake, 59
Public libraries, 31–32, 69, 74, 92, 97, 132–133

Quakers, 49, 93
Queen Elizabeth Way, 11, 26, 30, 32
Queen's Park, 5, 23, 106, 108, 111, 119
Queensville, 51–52

Radial railways, 17–18, 54, 70
Rattray Marsh Conservation Area, 34
Red Barn Theatre, 54–55
Rex Hotel, 92
Richmond Hill, 4, 36, 43, 69–73, 79
River Oaks, 25
Riverside, 89
Roach, Charles, 126
Robert McLaughlin Art Gallery, 110
Roosevelt Drive, 87
Rosebank, 85
Rosedale, 123
Rouge River, 58, 61, 70, 83, 119
Royal York Road, 131–132
Russian community, 6, 32, 73, 133
Ryerson University, 56

Salem Road, 91
San Francisco, 6–7, 32, 72, 122, 136
Sandford, 93
Sandhill, 39
Scarborough, 71, 119, 126–130, 135
Schomberg, 46
Scugog Township, 4, 81, 92, 99–103
Seattle, Washington, 136
Seneca College, 46
Shack, Eddie, 41
Sharon, 49–52
Sibbald Point Provincial Park, 55
Sibbald, Susan, 55–56
Simcoe Street, 97–98, 102, 110
Sixteen Mile Creek, 15, 24, 26
South Asian community, 32, 35, 78, 135
Speisman, Stephen, 135
Square One, 30–31, 34
St. Clair Avenue, 124–126
St. Lawrence River, 121
Stanley Avenue, 132–133
Station Road, 45
Steeles Avenue, 119, 130
Stockwell, Chris, 113
Stouffville, 57–59

Streetsville, 30, 32
Suburban downtowns, 30–32, 126–128, 133–136
Sunderland, 96, 98–99
Sutton, 55, 57

Terra Cotta, 39
Thomas, Jim, 60
Thornhill, 74, 77
Toronto, meaning of Mohawk word, 120
Toronto Passage, 61–62, 70, 133
Toronto Star, 115
Toronto Stock Exchange, 122
Toronto Street, 92
Toronto Township, 29–30, 32
Trafalgar Road, 24, 26
Twelve Mile Creek, 24, 26

Underground Railroad, 90
Unionville, 77
University Avenue, 120
University graduates, 25, 37, 78, 95
University of Toronto, 34, 71
Upper Canada Mall, 63
Upper Canada Place, 13, 63
Uxbridge, 4, 81, 91-95, 101–102, 134

Vancouver, 20, 72
Vaughan, 4, 36, 43, 69, 72–77, 102
Vaughan Road, 124
Villeneuve, Norman Marshall, 92
Virginia, Ontario, 55

West Indian community, 124–126
West Shore, 85
Westney Heights, 89
Whitby, 4, 81, 91, 102–107
Whitchurch-Stouffville, 4, 43, 57–61, 93
Wilson, David, 49–50, 52
Woodbridge, 74–76
Woodlands, 85
Wychwood Park, 80
Wyecroft Road, 26

Yonge Street, 59, 61–66, 69–70, 72, 120, 133
Yonge subway, 122, 133
York, City of, 119, 130
York Pioneer & Historical Society, 50

Zephyr, Ontario, 93

144